THE SUSPECT

THE SUSPECT
The Official Screenplay

STUART CONNELLY

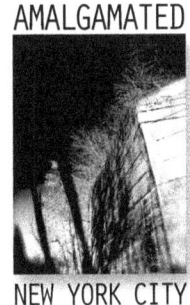

THE SUSPECT

Copyright © 2014 by The Suspect LLC

All rights reserved.

No part of this book may be reproduced in any form by electronic or mechanical means, including recording, photocopying, or digital information storage and retrieval without prior written permission from the copyright holder.

A portion of the Introduction to this book previously appeared in the *Huffington Post*.

Lyrics from *Black Bird Day* by Stephen Coates © 2012 Antique Beat. Used with kind permission of the artist.

Amalgamated Press
555 West 59th Street, Manhattan, New York 10019

Library of Congress Cataloging-in-Publication Data
    Connelly, Stuart
        Suspect, The / Stuart Connelly
          p. cm.
        ISBN-13: 978-0-988-89712-0
        ISBN-10: 0-988-89712-1
          1. confidence game – theft – counterfeiting
          2. crime – police – psychological thriller
          3. performing arts – motion pictures – screenplay
      I. Title

BOOK DESIGN BY TOPEKA
PHOTOGRAPHY BY SHERRY MCCRACKEN

Connect with the author at *www.stuartconnelly.com*

FIRST EDITION

Printed in the United States of America

10 9 8 7 6 5 4 3 2 1

ALSO BY STUART CONNELLY

NOVELS

Haven House

•

This Island, Made of Bone

•

Natural Selection (with Chad Scheifele)

•

Indelible

SHORT STORY COLLECTIONS

Matters of the Heart

•

Confessions of a Velour-Shirted Man

•

Evertheless

SCREENPLAYS

Cold-Hearted

•

In the Shadow of the Dream

•

Cousin Joey (with Sante D'Orazio)

NON-FICTION

Behind The Dream: The Making of the Speech That Transformed a Nation (with Clarence B. Jones)

•

Uprising: Understanding Attica, Revolution, And the Incarceration State (with Clarence B. Jones)

•

Dischord: Journeys into a Musical Mind (with Stephen Coates)

CONTENTS

INTRODUCTION　　　　　　　　　　　ix

THE SUSPECT SCREENPLAY　　　　　　1

CAST AND CREW CREDITS　　　　　114

INTRODUCTION

What you're holding in your hands is the shooting script for my debut as a feature film director. Which is not to say it's my first screenplay. I've written many others over the years, but the tale of Nathaniel Gray / Freeman Finch… something about my approach to his particular story… gave *The Suspect* script a kind of momentum beyond my previous efforts.

From the moment I started writing I saw how the film wanted, *needed* to look. My producing partner and wife Mary Jo believed in that vision, I "attached" myself as the director and our casting agent started shopping the script out to actors. And here was where the momentum kicked in: as the script made the rounds in New York and Hollywood, we starting getting enthusiastic response. And with it, a lot of requests for meetings with me (these actors are all well beyond the auditioning phase of their careers; you cast them by having conversations to see how you get along with each other).

It didn't take long to figure out exactly where this energy was coming from. Those actors were responding to a role they'd almost given up holding out hope to see. Without realizing it, I'd created the kind of character African-American actors rarely find: a nuanced, complicated, and intelligent lead. It's not a stretch to say we virtually had our pick of incredibly talented African-American men, all of whom wanted the opportunity to play this unusual and dynamic character.

But the idea that the fictional character I'd created slaked some deep-seated thirst for self-expression for a group of actors who are too often marginalized or typecast wasn't lost on me. It informed both my style of direction and my dedication to getting the film in front of the widest possible audience. In fact, part of why I decided to publish this screenplay was to offer a way for those who have seen the film to consider the character and theme on a more intimate scale.

The Suspect may seem like a message movie to some. Perhaps that's a good thing, although the very idea smacks of medicine rather than entertainment. I'd prefer that it be considered a particular kind of ride; a psychological thriller designed to entertain the audience and keep them guessing, but unlike most rides, you don't get off the same place you got on.

While it's truly painful for me to contemplate, I fully understand that the film owes its very existence to the ongoing problem of race relations in America. Like Quentin Tarantino's *D'Jango Unchained*, Ryan Coogler's *Fruitvale Station*, and Steve McQueen's *Twelve Years a Slave*, my film comes into the world at the expense – on the backs – of so many human beings who have suffered under the cruelty of institutionalized slavery and its long, echoing shadow; American-style racism. Racial tension is plot, is character, is environment, is theme in *The Suspect*.

The truth of the matter makes me feel a bit conflicted, though this conflict is nothing new, of course; tragedy of all sorts has always been the raw material for drama. As long as there has been human misery, there have been storytellers mining it. This is the unrelenting truth for any artist. The only question is, is the art we make from it of any use?

Still, of all the absurd things to tear at the fabric of society... The color of someone's skin? That pathetic, reptile-brain knee-jerk is our undoing? It's embarrassing. And yet this embarrassment is the central irony that circumscribes the problem. Those who are fundamentally opposed to racism don't want to dignify any aspect of it with discussion. So no one ends up talking about the realities of racial conflict, and in not talking we somehow feel the wounds will simply heal themselves. The fact of the matter is different: those wounds fester, and infection spreads.

For my part, I've always felt that each and every conversation about race, no matter how painful or awkward, is a stepping-stone toward some better understanding and a solution to the primal problem. Yes, it is a sensitive subject. Yes, we tend to get awfully quiet around it for fear of saying the wrong thing. But conversation, like therapy, is its own sort of "talking cure." I, for one, want to talk it out. *The Suspect* is a natural extension of that drive.

Before I was given the wonderful honor of co-writing with Dr. Clarence B. Jones his memoir of the Civil Rights Movement and the 1963 March on Washington (*Behind The Dream: The Making of the Speech that Transformed a Nation*; Palgrave Macmillan, 2011) I wrote a screenplay that covered his entire life story. Now, Clarence was born in 1930, so I struggled with the shifting language of the black / white issue decade-by-decade, finding the right phrase in the spectrum from "casual" racism to vehement hatred for the 30s, the 40s, the 50s and so on. The sheer breadth of the language was shocking. Every time I typed one of those words, I felt some kind of guilt by association.

I wanted to apologize to Clarence when I handed over my draft.

"This isn't me," I wanted to say. "This isn't how *I* look at the world."

I wanted to tell him I was sorry on behalf of all white people. But ever-so-slowly, I realized my hesitation was meaningless. Clarence had heard all those words before. He'd lived through my script for real. And nothing this writer – who was only trying to put Clarence's experience into a thematic context – could say would offend him in the slightest. He understood my intentions. In that light, those words that littered my script lost all their power to intimidate, to debase, to scar.

Understood intentions. A safe perch from which to explore the issue of race. Honest dialogue. My hope is that *The Suspect* – by placing racial tension, rage and misunderstanding center stage – will leverage the power of cinema to personalize and elevate the current conversation about race relations in America. My small contribution to the Movement.

Stuart Connelly
February 1, 2014

The time setting of **The Suspect** is purposely ambiguous --
a fusion of present and living-memory past.

Certain elements seem lifted from the early and mid-60s. The
police uniforms have a whiff of that Canadian Mountie flair,
the telephones have coiled cords and dials.

Others elements skew toward the late 70s and early 80s.
Vehicles are boxy steel behemoths, videotape and security
technology appears in its grainy black-and-white infancy.

Still others feel fully modern day.

All production design follows out of this ambiguity...

THE SUSPECT

written by
Stuart Connelly

CONTACT:

Mary Jo Barthmaier
Modoc Spring

Scott Aronson
Melee Entertainment

"THE SUSPECT"

FADE IN:

INT. LIVING ROOM -- MORNING

A woman in her late 30s, SHANNON -- all red hair and brown-eyed sadness -- reads quietly on her sofa.

EXT. PORCH, SUBURBAN HOUSE -- MORNING

A sun-dappled house. Autumn leaves drift down everywhere.

The silence is broken by the sudden appearance of a DELIVERY VEHICLE -- a motorcycle with a sidecar filled with packages.

INT. LIVING ROOM -- MORNING

Shannon is interrupted by a knock on the door.

EXT. PORCH, SUBURBAN HOUSE -- MORNING

Shannon opens her door to an OVERNIGHT DELIVERY MAN.

>   OVERNIGHT DELIVERY MAN
>   Good morning, ma'am.

The Delivery Man hands her a 9x12 cardboard envelope. She takes it with a smile as thin as the wispy envelope.

>   SHANNON
>   (considering)
>   It is, isn't it...?

>   OVERNIGHT DELIVERY MAN
>   (offering a clipboard)
>   I'll need a signature for this one.

Shannon signs the form.

>   OVERNIGHT DELIVERY MAN
>   Have a nice day.

Lost in thought, Shannon closes the door in the man's face.

INT. FOYER -- THAT MOMENT

Shannon hesitates at the door. Studies the envelope for too long, almost as if she's afraid to learn what's inside.

Then she heads up the stairs.

INT. MASTER BEDROOM -- MOMENTS LATER

Shannon sits down on her bed, still holding the sealed envelope. Her cheeks streaked with tears.

Building up the nerve.

As Shannon yanks the envelope's pull-tab open with the savage intensity of a woman pulling the rip-chord on a parachute that just might save her life, we --

                                                    FADE OUT.

EXT. MIDLAND TOWNSHIP BUILDING -- DAY

Scorching summer. Brooding skies. But everything's quiet.

A hulking police cruiser with a WINCH on the front end sits parked in front of an old stone building, big as a barn. Large hand printed lettering on the gable end reads:

  "MIDLAND TWP."

SUPER OPTICAL: "TWO MONTHS AGO"

SHERIFF DIXON, a brush-cut good 'ol boy in his 60s, climbs out from the driver's side, snuffs out his cigar, and heads inside...

OPENING CREDITS UNWIND to eerily upbeat, antiquated strains of music. The song is muffled as if emanating from an ill-tuned radio somewhere in the building.

MOVING THROUGH the front door, into --

INT. BULLPEN AREA, MIDLAND TOWNSHIP BUILDING -- THAT MOMENT

A drab, open area. A couple desks, some low cubicles beyond.

TRACKING INTO THE ROOM WITH SHERIFF DIXON

past HEATHER (late teens), a receptionist who paces in front of her desk. She keeps throwing concerned glances behind her.

                    THE SUSPECT (O.S.)
               ...And I'm gonna keep on sayin' it! You
               got no right!

Behind the desks, a small closed door where the racket's coming from.

                    HEATHER
               He's been keepin' on, Sheriff.

                    SHERIFF DIXON
               Riley wait for me then?

                    HEATHER
               'Course he would, you know better.

INT. CELL, MIDLAND TOWNSHIP BUILDING -- DAY

A VIDEO CAMERA VIEWFINDER IMAGE

with the tiny flashing "REC" graphic in the lower corner.

A PAIR OF EYES COME SLOWLY INTO FOCUS. Angry, blinking back tears. An African-American man, late 30s. THE SUSPECT.

                    THE SUSPECT
               That thing best be on! Yo, you
               recording this, my man? You better be.
               My lawyer'll be mighty interested in
               that there tape.

                    DEPUTY RILEY (O.S.)
               You're all set, sheriff.

                    SHERIFF DIXON (O.S.)
               Thanks much, Riley.

The camcorder ZOOMS OUT TO A WIDER SHOT, revealing --

The Suspect, handcuffed and seated in a small wooden chair. His light gray T-shirt streaked with mud. Sweat rings at the neck and armpits.

Sheriff Dixon moves a metal table in front of the Suspect. Then he gets one glass of water for himself, pulls over a matching chair and sits down opposite the Suspect.

                    SHERIFF DIXON
                         (to the Suspect)
               See, nice and cozy. Now we can talk.

                    THE SUSPECT
          You're going to sweat me, is that
          it? If you're gonna sweat me, why don't
          you take me into the box, like I see on
          TV.

                    SHERIFF DIXON
          That where you see "the box," on TV?
          Well, afraid this is the best we can do
          for you. Don't have much call for an
          interrogation room in this township.
               (sips some water, thinking)
          Don't have much call for days like
          today in this township, come to think
          about it.

FLASH ON --

INT. CAROLINA CREDIT & TRUST -- DAY //EARLIER//

Chaos.

A ski-masked BANK ROBBER waving a .45 PISTOL around, in the thick of it, as terrified FARMER CUSTOMERS and BANK EMPLOYEES cower in every corner.

                    THE BANK ROBBER
          I'm not FUCKING AROUND!

INT.   CELL, MIDLAND TOWNSHIP BUILDING -- BACK TO SCENE

The video camera viewfinder POV is gone, replaced by a

WIDE SHOT ON THE CELL

Cramped, but very clean. The camcorder sits in one corner on a tripod, red light glowing.

The STEEL-CAGE BARRED JAIL CELL sits in the corner of a huge shadow-crossed cinder block catch-all storage room. Filing cabinets and farm implements line the walls. Industrial sacks of ice-melting salt pellets and weed-killer.

Shafts of light, freedom, shine from one lone, high window.

DEPUTY RILEY, late 20s, skinny and desperately sincere, steps before the camera lens.

                    DEPUTY RILEY
               (to the camcorder)
          August 8th. The time is 3:10 p.m.
          Location, Midland Township Hall.
          Conversation with person of interest
          regarding the armed robbery of Carolina
          Credit and Trust at approximately one
          p.m. today. Interview conducted by
          Sheriff Amiel Dixon, name of
          interviewee is...

The deputy looks over. Sheriff Dixon stares at the Suspect.

                    SHERIFF DIXON
          Can you give the boy your name?

                    THE SUSPECT
          I don't recall you or your deputy here
          reading me my rights.

                    SHERIFF DIXON
          Come on, this is a friendly chat.
          Anyway, you probably know I can hold
          you without any charges for forty-eight
          hours.

                    THE SUSPECT
          Doesn't mean I have to say a
          motherfuckin' word.

Riley still stands in front of the camera, frozen smile plastered on.

                    SHERIFF DIXON
          No. No, it doesn't. But a), this here's
          a proper community of good Christian
          folk and we can do nicely without your
          urban profanity --

                    THE SUSPECT
               (interrupting)
          Urban?

                    SHERIFF DIXON
          -- and b), like you say, your lawyer
          will want to review our records, he'll
          see we're trying to follow good
          procedure here.

Sheriff Dixon casually stretches a hand out toward Deputy Riley, inviting the Suspect to help move things along.

SHERIFF DIXON
Your name's not going to be held against you.

The Suspect looks over at the camera.

THE SUSPECT
Freeman Finch.

DEPUTY RILEY
(hesitating)
Is that last name first, or --

THE SUSPECT
(interrupting)
Goddamn it. What'd I just say? You asked me my name.

SHERIFF DIXON
Hey, go easy on the boy.

DEPUTY RILEY
(to camcorder, flustered)
Interviewee, black adult male, carried no ID at time of apprehension. Interviewee alleges his name to be Finch Freeman.

SHERIFF DIXON
We never heard a name like that around here.
(to Riley)
Except like that actor. He's good.

DEPUTY RILEY
Yeah, he's a good one.

SHERIFF DIXON
You can trust a guy like that.

THE SUSPECT
(low, the trouble sinking in now)
Did you say "armed robbery" before?

SHERIFF DIXON
(pretending not to hear)
People around here have pretty plain handles. I can practically count the family names on one hand. Marshall. Beam. Let's see, you got Laird, you got...

A look to Deputy Riley for help.

DEPUTY RILEY
Noble.

SHERIFF DIXON
Noble. Noble family owns half the acreage around these parts. No Freemans.
    (beat)
Lot of times in prison, inmates are taught to give their last names first.

THE SUSPECT
In the military, too.

SHERIFF DIXON
That where you learned it?

THE SUSPECT
I didn't give you my first name last.

SHERIFF DIXON
How's that?

THE SUSPECT
You've got it backwards. I'm Freeman Finch. Mr. Finch.

SHERIFF DIXON
Hmmmm. Is that right?
    (to Riley)
First videotaped interview in township history and we got the intro wrong.
    (to the Suspect)
Well, afraid you're not so free now, Mr. Finch. Let's get down to clay here. You answer a few questions, we'll see if we can get you on your way back home, wherever you came from.

THE SUSPECT
Can I have some water?

SHERIFF DIXON
Due time. You thirsty, Freeman?

THE SUSPECT
I'm... Yeah, my throat's dry.

>   SHERIFF DIXON
>   All that digging? Hmmm?

FLASH ON --

EXT. FARM ROAD -- DAY //EARLIER//

Riley's police cruiser is pulled over. The deputy stands on the road's shoulder, hands on his hips, tense. He looks over the Suspect through squinted eyes.

>   DEPUTY RILEY
>   You don't mind me asking where the
>   dirt's from, do you?
>
>   THE SUSPECT
>   I'm looking at some land. I wanted to
>   see what it was like, how rich it was.

Deputy Riley's eyes are cold.

>   DEPUTY RILEY
>   Test it, you mean.
>
>   THE SUSPECT
>   Well, yeah. Test it in my own way.
>
>   DEPUTY RILEY
>   No pH testing or anything too...
>   complex, is that it?
>
>   THE SUSPECT
>   I wanted to see how dark it was.
>
>   DEPUTY RILEY
>   (nodding)
>   Okay, okay.
>   (beat)
>   Is it dark enough for you? Real jet
>   black soil?

INT.   CELL, MIDLAND TOWNSHIP BUILDING -- BACK TO SCENE

Deputy Riley pours a cup of water from the sweating pitcher. Takes a drink for himself.

                    SHERIFF DIXON (O.S.)
               I need to lay out the facts for you,
               son, so you get an idea of what you're
               up against.

                    THE SUSPECT (O.S.)
               I _know_ what I'm up against.

ANGLE ON THE TABLE

Dixon looks like he's trying to keep cool, and fighting his nature to do it. Riley pulls up a chair and sits between his boss and the man he's brought in.

                    SHERIFF DIXON
               This is a small town, and we ain't
               never had a bank robbery before.

                    DEPUTY RILEY
               It's a first, all right.

                    SHERIFF DIXON
               And you show up out of nowhere,
               Freeman. That's gotta raise a flag.

                    THE SUSPECT
               I suppose you're going to tell me I
               look just like the guy.

FLASH ON --

INT. CAROLINA CREDIT & TRUST -- DAY //EARLIER//

The Bank Robber flails around, using his out-of-control behavior as its own weapon, inciting panic.

The ski mask obscures his face, but the HAND gripping the pistol gives it away... the Bank Robber is African-American.

INT.   CELL, MIDLAND TOWNSHIP BUILDING -- BACK TO SCENE

                    SHERIFF DIXON
               Jury's still out on that one.

                    THE SUSPECT
               So you pick up a guy who's looking to
               perhaps buy property in this town, add
               to your goddamn tax base --

SHERIFF DIXON
(interrupting)
Language, now.

THE SUSPECT
-- because he's walking along the side of the road and you've never seen him before? Are you telling me that?

DEPUTY RILEY
Well the criminal's not going to be one of the townspeople now, is it?

THE SUSPECT
Why's that? No one's desperate here, these farmers? Diesel more than three bucks a gallon? The spread I'm looking at's in foreclosure.

SHERIFF DIXON
None of my citizens did this.

THE SUSPECT
How do you know? If you think I'm guilty you can't be too squared away about the situation.
(sorting things out for himself)
The guy who did it was a brother, that's obvious. You're narrowing things down.

The two policemen share a look. Sheriff Dixon's eyes seem to say: You made your bed, now lie in it.

But the deputy won't cough up the truth.

The Suspect can see it anyway, though. Clear as day.

THE SUSPECT
You can't be serious...

SHERIFF DIXON
(to Riley)
Why don't you get the man his water now?

But Riley doesn't budge.

                    THE SUSPECT
          Ah, no, you cannot tell me there are no
          black people in this town.

                    DEPUTY RILEY
          Well there's currently one around here.
          Whoever made a four-hundred-and-sixty-
          one thousand dollar withdrawal from our
          bank.

                    THE SUSPECT
          And there's me. So that's two.

The sheriff takes over the task the deputy won't do and pours a
cup of water for the Suspect.

                    SHERIFF DIXON
          But to answer your question, none of
          the people who live here are African-
          American. Unless you're making an offer
          on that farm you saw today.

                    THE SUSPECT
          If this is the Welcome Wagon...

Dixon returns to the table.

                    SHERIFF DIXON
          C'mon now, wouldn't you call our
          exchange very civil?
                    (handing the cup of water
                     over)
          See, we're not sweating you.

The Suspect raises his cuffed wrists.

                    THE SUSPECT
          These say different.

                    SHERIFF DIXON
          Those? For your own safety.

The Suspect downs the water in a few gulps. He's forced to hold
both hands to his face because of the handcuffs.

                    SHERIFF DIXON
          Freeman, you may want to look at this
          from our angle. You're not from around
          these parts, you've got no ID on you,
          no car, you're covered with dirt like
          you've been out digging --

                    DEPUTY RILEY
               (interrupting)
          Burying something, maybe.

                    SHERIFF DIXON
          -- and to top it all off...

Dixon catches himself and stops mid-thought.

                    THE SUSPECT
          To top it all off what?

The sheriff stays quiet.

                    THE SUSPECT
          What?

                    DEPUTY RILEY
          What he means is on top of everything
          we've got this armed robbery deal.

                    THE SUSPECT
               (eyes never leaving Dixon's)
          No, no, you were talking about me, not
          the town. I'm not from here, I'm
          covered with dirt, and to top it all
          off I'm... what?

                    SHERIFF DIXON
          Now son...

The Suspect suddenly rises, furious.

                    THE SUSPECT
          Say it!

In an instant, Riley and Dixon are on their feet. The deputy
DRAWS HIS GUN.

                    DEPUTY RILEY
          Sit down! Right now.

                    THE SUSPECT
          I'm black. Say it!

                    DEPUTY RILEY
          Don't you make me shoot.

                    SHERIFF DIXON
               (shaken)
          Don't you make him shoot now!

                    THE SUSPECT
          I'm handcuffed, I'm in a jail cell.

                    DEPUTY RILEY
          You are threatening peace officers
          right now, and that's on tape. Now sit
          DOWN!

                    THE SUSPECT
          Not until he says it. You want to shoot
          me on camera, shoot me.
               (to the sheriff)
          You say what you were going to say.

Dixon's eyes move to the camcorder, the deputy's gun, the
Suspect. A triangle. Over and over. Like he's in a standoff.

A RUMBLE OF THUNDER rolls in the distance.

EXT.   HIGHWAY, OUTSKIRTS OF MIDLAND -- DAY

Beneath a flash of heat lightning and the same ECHO OF THUNDER,
a BEATEN-UP SILVER SEDAN motors along the two-lane. As it
passes, the driver's appearance becomes clear.

He's African-American. He's THE BANK ROBBER.

INT.   SILVER SEDAN //MOVING// -- THAT MOMENT

Does the Bank Robber look like the Suspect? Same age, similar
build, same skin color. Other than that, they're clearly two
different men of the same race.

The Bank Robber keeps one hand protectively on the car seat next
to him. Right on top of the DUFFLE BAG OF STOLEN MONEY.

INT.   CELL, MIDLAND TOWNSHIP BUILDING -- DAY

The Suspect is still on his feet.

                    DEPUTY RILEY
          You want to get shot over this?

                    THE SUSPECT
          I like my odds. You haven't charged me
          with shit, I'm innocent, and the only
          thing I'm doing is standing up.

SHERIFF DIXON
All I was going to say was that you're not dressed like a man looking at real estate.

THE SUSPECT
Bullshit.
(to Riley)
I'll tell you one thing, deputy, if you shoot you're going to want to burn that videotape there, 'cause it'll bury you.

The two cops share another look. They're out of their depth and they know it.

SHERIFF DIXON
Okay. Okay. What I was going to say, yes, I see you're black. Riley sees that, and the man we're looking for is black. Call that racist if you want...

THE SUSPECT
No, I call it logical. It's the fact that we all look alike to you that's racist.

SHERIFF DIXON
Hey! Neither of us were at the bank. You fit the description of the perpetrator. Plain and simple.

Dixon's back in control.

SHERIFF DIXON
This isn't worth the walls of Jericho tumbling down. It should be a civil talk. It's not worth a tragic ending.

He reaches out and carefully pushes Riley's gun barrel down until it's aimed at the floor.

SHERIFF DIXON
Now will you sit down? Because it's very easy for you to get all high and mighty about profiling and the like, but in the meantime, you're the best explanation we have for a very serious crime. I'm sorry if that scares you.

THE SUSPECT
It doesn't scare me, it makes me sick.

                    DEPUTY RILEY
               (to Sheriff Dixon)
          I don't understand why you're being so
          nice to him, sir.

                    SHERIFF DIXON
               (still looking at   the
               Suspect)
          Because he's our guest. And because we
          don't know he's done anything wrong
          yet.

The deputy glares at the Suspect. He knows differently.

                    THE SUSPECT
          And what exactly do you mean
          by "yet?"

                    SHERIFF DIXON
               (to the Suspect)
          Thing is, you gotta admit, there's a
          lot of explaining you have to do.

                    THE SUSPECT
          No there's not. You ever heard of a
          little concept called innocent 'til
          proven guilty?

                    SHERIFF DIXON
          And just how do you think people like
          us prove people like you are guilty? We
          piece together evidence. Like it is
          evident very few men walk around
          without a wallet --

                    THE SUSPECT
               (interrupting)
          I told you, my wallet's in my car --

                    SHERIFF DIXON
               (interrupting)
          And your car's gone missing, I know,
          we've heard that.

                    THE SUSPECT
          I broke down, I walked to the property
          I wanted to see, and by the time I got
          back, the car had either been towed --

                    DEPUTY RILEY
                (interrupting)
            We called every wrecking yard in the
            county.

                    THE SUSPECT
            -- or stolen. That seems impossible to
            you?

                    SHERIFF DIXON
            Given the circumstances? If not
            impossible then at least one heck of a
            coincidence.

                    THE SUSPECT
            Coincidences happen.

                    SHERIFF DIXON
            Do they? I'd say that's for juries to
            determine.

                    THE SUSPECT
            Wow. Unbelievable.
                (to himself)
            "The Court wants nothing from you. It
            receives you when you come and it
            dismisses you when you go."

                    SHERIFF DIXON
            Oh look, got a reader here. This is
            straight outta Kafka, you're saying?

The Suspect struggles to keep his surprise in check. Riley's doing some of the same, but hides it with a beaming smile, as if to say: See that? We're not just a bunch of backwoods hicks here.

                    SHERIFF DIXON
            Now we're getting somewhere. Breaking
            down stereotypes and the like. Except I
            think you're some gang-banger only
            knows Kafka 'cause of some rap song,
            and you think I only know about him
            'cause... I don't know... it was
            assigned reading in Klan College.

The Suspect almost laughs at that.

                    SHERIFF DIXON
            But the truth is, there's more going on
            with you than I'll ever know. You're
            smarter than I'm giving you credit for.
                (MORE)

                    SHERIFF DIXON (CONT'D)
          Same goes for me. And this here meeting
          isn't about existential confusion, it's
          about a crime I have every intention of
          solving.

                    THE SUSPECT
          You have no idea what this
          is about.

The Suspect's focus drifts toward the cell door as Heather
appears on the other side of the bars.

                    HEATHER
          Sheriff? Meredith's here for you.

LATER --

The police are gone. The Suspect sits alone in the cell,
shackled hands on the table drumming his fingers.

A glance over to the camcorder. The red light under the lens is
no longer glowing. The Suspect gets up, goes over to the bars.
Looks out, strains to hear.

[Dialogue bleeds in from next scene, barely audible]

INT.   RECEPTION AREA, MIDLAND TOWNSHIP BUILDING -- THAT MOMENT

MEREDITH, plump, 50, one of the bank tellers, has fear stitched
into her face.

                    SHERIFF DIXON
          ...frightening for you. Look at how a
          day can suddenly break wide open. Into
          violence...

                    MEREDITH
          I really just want to go home.
              (beat)
          Or maybe to see Dr. Coleson. Yeah. My
          heart's still pounding.

                    SHERIFF DIXON
          You have to do this, Meredith. The man
          pointed a gun in your face --

                    MEREDITH
              (interrupting)
          That's exactly the problem, Amiel!
          You're asking me to act as if it's all
          just another --

From down the hall, the Suspect's voice bounces off the building's plaster walls.

                THE SUSPECT (O.S.)
  Hey!

Fear flickers in Meredith's eyes.

The sheriff ignores the plea.

                SHERIFF DIXON
  This kind of thing doesn't go on in
  Midland. No one can think that it does.
  It can't go unanswered. We stand up for
  ourselves.

                THE SUSPECT (O.S.)
    (echoing)
  Hey!

                HEATHER
  I'll go see what he needs.

                SHERIFF DIXON
    (to Heather)
  He doesn't need anything. He's making a
  fuss because he's caught.

                DEPUTY RILEY
  Like a rat in a trap.

                HEATHER
  He's in our custody and he's crying
  out. You two are tied up, don't you
  think someone should check on him?

Reluctantly, the sheriff sees her point.

                SHERIFF DIXON
  Don't get too close.

Dixon turns back to Meredith as Heather exits.

                SHERIFF DIXON
  You need to see him and make an
  identification.

                MEREDITH
  We have the security tape.

                SHERIFF DIXON
  It doesn't show us enough.

                    MEREDITH
          Whatever the camera saw is what I saw.
          Only better, because unlike the camera,
          I was watching through tears!

                    SHERIFF DIXON
          Listen. Meredith: You need to look at
          this man who pointed a gun at you and
          tell us he's the one.

Meredith looks between the two policemen.

                    MEREDITH
          You're sure he *is* the one?

INT. CELL, MIDLAND TOWNSHIP BUILDING -- THAT MOMENT

Heather steps over to the bars, cautious. She looks in at the
Suspect, sitting on the corner of the table.

                    HEATHER
          Are you in distress?

                    THE SUSPECT
          What? In *what*?

                    HEATHER
          Distress?

The Suspect comes over to the door and faces off with Heather,
the bars dividing them.

                    THE SUSPECT
          Who the fuck talks that way?

The word stings like a slap.

                    HEATHER
          It... it means --

                    THE SUSPECT
             (interrupting)
          I know what it means. What kind of
          manual told you to use a word like
          that? You people must think you're some
          kind of big city outfit. "Distress."
          All NYPD Blue.

                    HEATHER
          If you're not in distress --

                    THE SUSPECT
                  (interrupting)
               I am an innocent man behind bars due to
               the simple fact that I'm black. That
               shit is distressing
               by definition.

Heather clears her throat, boosting up her nerve.

                    HEATHER
               What I'm saying, you were crying out.
               If you're in immediate danger or
               require medical assistance, I'm allowed
               to help you. Otherwise...

She doesn't belabor the obvious by finishing her explanation.

The Suspect takes her in with a long calculating look.

                    THE SUSPECT
               Otherwise you're not stepping foot in
               here, huh? I need to be having some
               kind of seizure.

Heather doesn't answer.

                    THE SUSPECT
               What's your name?

With that question, it's as if Heather has broken through. She almost glows when she answers:

                    HEATHER
               Heather. What's yours?

And then, the crushing response. Not a name in return, but:

                    THE SUSPECT
               They talking about the color of my skin
               out there, Heather? They are, aren't
               they?

Before Heather can answer -- if she even knows *how* to answer, how to hide the hurt -- Deputy Riley approaches.

                    DEPUTY RILEY
               Everything okay back here?

No one says anything.

The deputy's eyes land on the camcorder.

The red light is BACK ON.

And the camera's been twisted on its tripod so it's facing the doorway where the Suspect and Heather are talking.

>   DEPUTY RILEY
>   What in the world?
>   (to the Suspect, pointing at
>   the camcorder)
>   Did you turn that on?

>   THE SUSPECT
>   Well it's not like it turned on
>   by itself.

>   DEPUTY RILEY
>   You can't do that.

>   THE SUSPECT
>   Why not? It's here to record what
>   happens while I'm in custody, right?
>   Just because you're not back here
>   doesn't mean I'm not still
>   in custody.

The deputy fumbles with his keyring.

>   THE SUSPECT
>   Doesn't matter if you see me or not.
>   I'm here. You guys have a problem with
>   object permanence?

>   DEPUTY RILEY
>   The camera is here to record the
>   interview, something Miss Noble has
>   nothing to do with.

>   THE SUSPECT
>   You mean Heather?

Deputy Riley tries to let that comment bounce off him.

He finds the jail key and pushes Heather out of the way as he unlocks the bars.

>   THE SUSPECT
>   Hey, I saw that. Police brutality.

>   DEPUTY RILEY
>   Shut up.

Riley slips into the cell, slamming the door behind him, and heads for the tripod.

The Suspect stays close to Heather. They both watch as the deputy turns the camera off and unscrews it from its mount.

Taking his video camera with him, Riley returns to the cell door and unlocks it again, heading back out.

> THE SUSPECT
> What are you trying to hide?

> DEPUTY RILEY
> What are <u>you</u> trying to pull?

Riley slips through and closes the cell door behind him.

> DEPUTY RILEY
> (to Heather)
> Come on.

Heather gives the Suspect the quickest of looks -- is that honest sympathy in her eyes?

The spell is broken as she turns away. She and Riley walk out of the storage room together.

> THE SUSPECT
> (calling after)
> Hey, Heather! We'll talk later. Okay, sugar?

The Suspect's completely alone again. He looks around the barren cell.

INT. RECEPTION AREA, MIDLAND TOWNSHIP BUILDING -- MOMENTS LATER

Deputy Riley approaches Sheriff Dixon, who's still working on Meredith. Riley waves the camcorder in front of his boss.

> DEPUTY RILEY
> The prisoner was messing with our equipment.

The sheriff lets on he's frustrated. Why isn't anything easy?

> SHERIFF DIXON
> Did he erase anything?

> DEPUTY RILEY
> I don't think so. I think he was just... recording more.

The policemen look at each other, trying to figure out if this is somehow a negative. Maybe there's a blind spot here.

                    SHERIFF DIXON
    What's he trying to prove?

                    DEPUTY RILEY
    I don't know, sheriff. We're not doing
    anything wrong. I suppose he's just
    looking for a reaction.

                    SHERIFF DIXON
    Baiting us. I guess. We don't want to
    fall for any of that. Cool heads,
    right?

                    DEPUTY RILEY
    Yeah. Like I said, we're by the book on
    this one so far.

                    SHERIFF DIXON
    Even so, we have to keep on treading
    lightly.

Riley nods, in complete agreement.

                    SHERIFF DIXON
    And that business in there with your
    sidearm doesn't help.

                    DEPUTY RILEY
    Might maybe you take a run at him alone
    for a try? I steer clear?

The sheriff nods, as if it wasn't his idea all along.

                    SHERIFF DIXON
    That's good thinking, Riley.

INT. CELL, MIDLAND TOWNSHIP BUILDING -- LATER

The red light on the camcorder glows steadily.

Sheriff Dixon sits alone across from the Suspect. Both quietly regard each other. Finally:

                    THE SUSPECT
    You running the clock out?

                    SHERIFF DIXON
    How's that?

The Suspect tilts his head in the camcorder's direction.

> THE SUSPECT
> Only so much tape. Click, it gets to the end, it's open season.

> SHERIFF DIXON
> Open season. In what way?

> THE SUSPECT
> You know, the stuff comes out. The real you.

> SHERIFF DIXON
> We'll change that tape up quick as a wink, son. Got plenty in the supply closet.

> THE SUSPECT
> What did you call me?

> SHERIFF DIXON
> "Son."

> THE SUSPECT
> It wasn't "boy?" I thought it was.

> SHERIFF DIXON
> I think you're hearing things. Good thing the camera's on. We can double check.

> THE SUSPECT
> Yeah. Good thing.

> SHERIFF DIXON
> (in a sportscaster's voice)
> "Let's go to the videotape!"

No reaction.

Dixon clears his throat -- alright then, down to business.

> SHERIFF DIXON
> See, the thing is, Freeman, you're up against it. You can play cool, you can play the race card, but the fact remains.

> THE SUSPECT
> What fact is that?

SHERIFF DIXON
          The fact that our bank gets ripped off,
          and ten minutes later we find you -- a
          stranger, a man who has no business
          being in Midland -- walking along
          looking very suspicious.

                    THE SUSPECT
          Is that how I look to you? Like I have
          no business to take care of?

                    SHERIFF DIXON
          You know as well as I do you have only
          one reason for being in our little
          town.

                    THE SUSPECT
          Oh, I know as well as you, huh?

                    SHERIFF DIXON
          Why don't you save us all a lot of time
          and just admit that reason?

The Suspect thinks about that.

EXT. NORTHSTAR MOTEL, ST. PAUL -- MORNING //FLASHBACK//

A run-down place. The city's skyscrapers glisten in the b.g.

SUPER OPTICAL: "ONE WEEK EARLIER"

The Bank Robber and the Suspect step out of a motel room.
<u>Together</u>. They nearly run into a MAID pushing a cart.

                    THE BANK ROBBER
               (to the Maid)
          Hey. Do you know where Polaski is?

The Maid looks confused.

                    MAID
          I've heard of it. Maybe forty miles
          from here. You're not that close. You
          got to go south on 52.

                    THE BANK ROBBER
          Okay, thanks.

While he hands her a dollar The Suspect steps out of the motel
and pops the trunk of the silver sedan, which is parked right in

front of their room. He slips something in. Then the two men climb inside.

The car sports an Illinois license plate: "Land of Lincoln."

EXT. FARM ROAD, POLASKI -- DAY

The silver sedan pulls onto the shoulder right by a REAL ESTATE SIGN that's planted at the end of a long winding driveway:

>"LAND AUCTION
>40 ACRES OF PROPERTY
>EQUIPMENT AND FURNISHING"

The Bank Robber gets out from the passenger side, wearing jeans and a gray T-shirt. He comes around the driver's side.

The Suspect leans out the window from behind the wheel.

>THE SUSPECT
>You ready?

>THE BANK ROBBER
>Ready as I'll ever be.

The car pulls away, kicking up a cloud of dust.

The Bank Robber watches it go, then collects himself and heads up the driveway on foot.

EXT. ORION SAVINGS & LOAN, POLASKI -- DAY

The silver sedan pulls into a parking spot. The driver's door opens. The Suspect climbs out with an EMPTY DUFFLE BAG.

Then, getting his head in the game, he fishes a SKI MASK out of his jacket pocket and heads toward the bank door.

INT. ORION SAVINGS & LOAN, POLASKI -- MOMENTS LATER

The Suspect waves his gun around as the panicked TELLERS fill the duffle bag with cash.

>THE SUSPECT
>Let's go! Come on!

EXT. FARM, POLASKI -- DAY

A simple STONE FARMHOUSE and BARN.

The Bank Robber walks around, studying the place. He squats here and there, digging around in the soil with his bare hands, as if assessing its value.

Something catches his eye.

The little haunted-looking playground at the farm -- rusty slide, one swing moving forlornly in the summer breeze.

The Bank Robber looks around nervously, glances at his watch. Doing a little mental calculation, he realizes it's time to go.

Wiping his hands conspicuously on his gray shirt -- a final and carefully determined move -- he heads for the road.

EXT. POLASKI TOWN SQUARE -- DAY

The silver sedan whips along the blacktop, speeding away from the scene of the crime.

INT. ORION SAVINGS & LOAN SECURITY ROOM, POLASKI -- DAY

The POLASKI SHERIFF (a tense man in his mid-50s) studies the security camera tape of the robbery on the small black and white monitor.

He whistles at the sheer intensity of what he's seeing.

> POLASKI SHERIFF
> One bold son of a bitch.
> (to the other cops)
> Well look at this.

Some of the other POLICE OFFICERS gather around the screen.

> POLASKI SHERIFF
> Seems we're dealing with an undesirable element, boys.

The Polaski Sheriff pauses the tape,

ANGLE ON

the screen staring at the DARK SKIN of the Suspect's hand.

EXT. FARM ROAD -- DAY

The Bank Robber shuffles along the side of the road, aimlessly walking toward the flat horizon.

A Polaski POLICE CRUISER slows to a stop behind him, gravel crunching under its wheels. Two PATROL COPS get out. Weapons slide out of their holsters.

                    FIRST PATROL COP
        Sir! Stop your walking and turn around
        right now!

The Bank Robber does as he's told, interlocking his hands on the top of his head as he registers the guns pointed at him.

                    THE BANK ROBBER
        Just looking at some property in the
        area, officers.

The Second Cop leans in and grabs hold of the cruiser's radio.

                    SECOND PATROL COP
          (into mic)
        Sheriff? This is car four-two. Can you
        come in?

                    POLASKI SHERIFF (V.O.)
          (filtered through static)
        Go ahead, Ron.

                    SECOND PATROL COP
        We've found something.

INT. POLASKI GOVERNMENT CENTER -- DAY

The Bank Robber sits across from the Polaski Sheriff. One leg is manacled to the leg of the Sheriff's desk.

A CAMCORDER is running in the corner, set up on a tripod.

                    THE BANK ROBBER
        Why do you keep saying "boy?"

                    POLASKI SHERIFF
        I'm not calling you "boy," that's in
        your head.

                    THE BANK ROBBER
        The hell it is, sir. I heard you.

                    POLASKI SHERIFF
          If I did say that, and I don't think I
          did, I apologize. It's what I'm used to
          calling my son.

                    THE BANK ROBBER
          But he's not thirty-eight, is he?

                    POLASKI SHERIFF
          No.

                    THE BANK ROBBER
          It doesn't sit right with me, just
          hearing it. Maybe you don't mean
          anything by it, maybe you do. All I
          know is I get a white cop saying it to
          me, I react. Negatively.

The Polaski Sheriff shifts in his seat, as if to get a better look at the Bank Robber.

                    POLASKI SHERIFF
          All right. If we've cleared up the
          direct address issues, if we're PC,
          let's go over your story again.

                    THE BANK ROBBER
          It's not a story.

                    POLASKI SHERIFF
          Then let's go over your statement
          again. Sir.

Instead, the Bank Robber's statement is SPITTING in the sheriff's face.

INT. NORTHSTAR MOTEL ROOM -- DAY

The Suspect stands between twin beds, leaning in toward the night stand to answer the RINGING PHONE. He's wearing small wire-rim John Lennon glasses.

On the bed in the f.g., the duffle bag sits with the bank's money spilled out.

                    THE SUSPECT
               (into phone)
          Hello?

OPERATOR (V.O.)
(through phone)
Dr. Greer? This is the four o'clock reminder call you asked for.

THE SUSPECT
Yeah, thank you.

EXT. NORTHSTAR MOTEL, ST. PAUL -- DAY

The Suspect slams the lid of the silver sedan's trunk closed.

He opens the driver's side, carefully pushing the duffle bag through to the passenger seat in ahead of him. Then he gets behind the wheel.

INT. POLASKI GOVERNMENT CENTER -- DAY

The Bank Robber sits staring at the Polaski Sheriff, who's on a rant.

POLASKI SHERIFF
You want to know the chance of two niggers coming through my town on the same day?

THE BANK ROBBER
I don't need to know the chances. It happened. Unless the other guy was in blackface, I know it happened, 'cause I'm not the guy that robbed your bank.

POLASKI SHERIFF
I think you should consider telling me where you buried the money, boy. It'll make life a whole hell of a lot easier.

THE BANK ROBBER
There it is again. You can stop calling me boy.

POLASKI SHERIFF
Polite time is over. You come to my town, take what's not yours, lie? I'll call you whatever I want, boy. And that ain't the worst of it.

INT. ORION SAVINGS & LOAN, POLASKI -- DAY

Two police officers are studying the video playback of the robbery.

On the next monitor over, the silver sedan pulls into a parking spot near two police cars.

As the driver's door opens, several of the cops catch sight of it.

>   FIRST COP
>   Johnny!
>
>   SECOND COP
>   (not looking)
>   Yep?
>
>   FIRST COP
>   What do you make of this?

The Second Cop looks at the other monitor.

THE COPS' POV

As the Suspect gets out of the car, he lifts the duffle bag over his head with both hands, as if in surrender and starts to move toward the bank.

>   SECOND COP
>   The sheriff sure ain't going to believe
>   it.

Instantly the cops bolt toward the front door.

EXT. ORION SAVINGS & LOAN PARKING LOT, POLASKI -- DAY

The cops surround the Suspect, all pointing their guns.

The Suspect is splayed out on all fours, supplicating himself, completely non-threatening.

>   THE SUSPECT
>   I'm not armed.
>
>   FIRST COP
>   (to the other cops)
>   Holy geez. That's the duffle bag from
>   the security tape.

The First Cop kicks the bag, feels the give.

                    SECOND COP
                (to the Suspect)
            What's in there?

                    FIRST COP
            Johnny? This is... Christ, this is the
            money from the robbery.

                    THE SUSPECT
            He's right.

The First Cop cocks the hammer back on his gun.

                    FIRST COP
            I wasn't talking to you, boy.

The First Cop kicks the Suspect on the shoulder. His head jerks and his eyeglasses tumble to the ground.

                    THE SUSPECT
            You don't need to point that at me. I'm
            not a criminal.

                    SECOND COP
            No? What are you, then?

The Suspect hesitates a bit, nervous, tense.

                    THE SUSPECT
            I'm a college professor.

The cops all stare at each other, trying to add this mess up.

The First Cop bends down and unzips the corner of the bag. He can see the edge of a packet of fifty-dollar bills.

                    FIRST COP
            Better get the sheriff on the air.

INT. POLASKI GOVERNMENT CENTER -- DAY

The Polaski Sheriff is on the phone.

He eyes the Bank Robber as he absorbs information he's hearing that can't easily be sorted out.

                    POLASKI SHERIFF
                (into phone)
            Kersands University... Okay, Jesus. Let
            me process it all and get back to you.

The sheriff hangs up and looks over at the Bank Robber, who's looking back with a satisfied expression.

> THE BANK ROBBER
> Was that the bank? Did they get a deposit they weren't expecting?

> POLASKI SHERIFF
> (after a long study of his captive)
> What do you know about this returning of the money?

> THE BANK ROBBER
> Only everything.

Somehow, the sheriff isn't exactly surprised at this.

> POLASKI SHERIFF
> Well, we'd better elevate the conversation here then, hadn't we?

> THE BANK ROBBER
> It looks like the answers you're seeking are over at the bank, That'd be my first stop if I were you.

> POLASKI SHERIFF
> Would it?

> THE BANK ROBBER
> Have your conversation there.

> POLASKI SHERIFF
> And who would I be talking with?

> THE BANK ROBBER
> (a beat)
> Why don't I introduce you?

INT. ORION SAVINGS & LOAN, POLASKI -- LATER

The Suspect sits calmly at the Bank Manager's desk, hands cuffed in front of him.

The three cops surround him, eyeing him as if they half-expect he's going to disappear in a flash of smoke right before their eyes.

In the b.g., several tellers and a BANK MANAGER count out the packets of cash from the Suspect's duffle bag.

The Polaski Sheriff comes into the bank, dragging the Bank Robber along in handcuffs. He makes his way over to where the Suspect is sitting.

The Suspect and the Bank Robber let their eyes meet.

                    THE SUSPECT
              (to the Bank Robber)
Freeman.

                  THE BANK ROBBER
Arthur.

                  POLASKI SHERIFF
Okay, we better thresh everything out from the jump, and if it don't add up, there's hell to pay.

                  THE SUSPECT
              (to the Bank Robber, ignoring
               the sheriff)
You okay?

                  THE BANK ROBBER
Not too bad.

The Polaski Sheriff looks at the material on the desk.

                  POLASKI SHERIFF
What's all this?

TIGHT ON THE DESK

There are two different KERSANDS UNIVERSITY BUSINESS CARDS, A GUN, and a CASHIER'S CHECK.

                  THE SUSPECT
I can explain everything.

                  POLASKI SHERIFF
I'm not talking to you, I'm talking to my men.

                  SECOND COP
The gun's a toy, presumably that's what was used during the course of the
              (MORE)

                    SECOND COP (CONT'D)
          robbery. We're still going over the
          videotape to verify that.

                    THE SUSPECT
          I would never use a real gun.

                    SECOND COP
          The business cards, well, you can see
          for yourself.

The Polaski Sheriff picks up the business cards. Studies both of them for a long moment.

                    POLASKI SHERIFF
               (reading)
          "Arthur Greer, PhD."

                    THE SUSPECT
          That's me.

                    POLASKI SHERIFF
               (reading)
          "School of Social Sciences."

                    THE SUSPECT
          Specifically, the Department of Social
          Psychology. And of course you already
          know my associate, Freeman Finch.
          Freeman's with the African-American
          Studies program.

The Bank Robber holds out his cuffed hands to shake.

The sheriff stares him down. Contemplates what he's dealing with here. He looks between the two black men.

                    THE SUSPECT
          Ladies and gentlemen, we'd like to
          share some news with you. You're all
          part of an unique experiment in racial
          dynamics and bias.

The Bank Manager comes over from behind the teller counter.

                    BANK MANAGER
          It's all here. Every dollar.

The Suspect moves his hands toward the desk and all the police freak out, tensing and reaching for their holsters.

                    SECOND COP
          Don't you move!

The Suspect freezes, hands hovering just a few inches above the
cashier's check.

                    THE BANK ROBBER
          I was just going to show you that
          check. It's made out to your township
          and it should cover the costs of the
          day.

                    POLASKI SHERIFF
          The day...

                    THE BANK ROBBER
          You know: gas, wear and tear on the
          vehicles, the videotape, maybe overtime
          involved.

The Second Cop still has his gun out.

                    SECOND COP
          Ammunition.

                    POLASKI SHERIFF
          Put the gun away, Johnny.

                    THE SUSPECT
          The university is very sensitive to the
          opportunity costs of involving law
          enforcement.

                    POLASKI SHERIFF
          Let me get this straight. You saying
          we're on some kind of Candid Camera?

                    THE BANK ROBBER
          Not at all. It isn't a joke, sheriff.
          It's incredibly important social
          research.

                    THE SUSPECT
          But to answer your question, yeah, you
          were the victim of a very elaborate,
          orchestrated illusion. It's for the
          greater good.

The Suspect holds his cuffed wrists out gently.

THE SUSPECT
Why don't you take these things off and the three of us can go back to your office. We can explain everything to you there.

POLASKI SHERIFF
We could do that, or I could run you boys in for malicious misuse of public services, inciting a riot, endangering public safety --

THE SUSPECT
(interrupting)
We can debate the merits of our methodology all you want, sir. The fact is, this is a social experiment that necessitated people feel they were in danger.

THE BANK ROBBER
We've returned the money, no one was hurt, and none of the other communities we've visited has found it necessary to file charges.

POLASKI SHERIFF
You've done this another place?

THE SUSPECT
Several, yes. And we always alert the state police beforehand.

THE BANK ROBBER
Officer, this is a high level sociological experiment.

POLASKI SHERIFF
About what?

THE BANK ROBBER
(low)
You don't want to discuss that here, sheriff.

THE SUSPECT
Why don't we go somewhere and talk this over like civilized people?

He leans in close, so only the sheriff can hear.

> THE SUSPECT
> You don't need the busy-bodies around here knowing your dirty beliefs and darkest secrets.

INT. POLASKI SHERIFF'S CAR //MOVING// -- DAY

The Polaski Sheriff drives.

The Bank Robber and the Suspect are in back, speaking quietly to each other.

> THE SUSPECT
> How were they with the tape?

> THE BANK ROBBER
> It wasn't a fight at all. They see themselves a certain way, there's no objective view of behavior.

> THE SUSPECT
> Do you think we should review it with them, or is it --

> POLASKI SHERIFF
> (interrupting)
> You want to let us know what's going on with this experiment, so we can decide how bad to ream you?

The Bank Robber leans forward to talk with the sheriff.

> THE BANK ROBBER
> It's pretty simple.

> THE SUSPECT
> I think we should wait until we get to the station, Freeman.

> POLASKI SHERIFF
> You best come clean while I'm in a good mood, gentlemen. It's five minutes to town hall, I think I'd better have a handle on what kind of hell you've raised in my backyard before we get there.

The two prisoners look at each other. Silently assessing the situation. Something passes between them.

>   THE SUSPECT
> We'll wait until we see the tape.
>
>   POLASKI SHERIFF
> What the hell for? There's nothing on
> that tape.
>
>   THE SUSPECT
> How do you know?
>
>   POLASKI SHERIFF
> Because I was there.
>
>   THE SUSPECT
> With all respect, sometimes people
> don't see the way the camera does.

INT. POLASKI GOVERNMENT CENTER -- DAY

The Suspect, the Polaski Sheriff and the Bank Robber huddle around a TV set.

A frozen image of the Bank Robber at the very desk they're standing at stares out at the men.

The Suspect hits the "PAUSE" button, starting up the image.

>   THE BANK ROBBER
>   (on TV)
> There it is again. You can stop calling
> me boy.

The Suspect hits "PAUSE" again, and the picture freezes.

>   THE SUSPECT
>   (to the Polaski Sheriff)
> You're upset, I can see that. So the
> first thing I want to stress is this
> experiment is in no way designed to
> point fingers at individuals.
>
>   THE BANK ROBBER
> We've performed this same scenario in a
> dozen small towns throughout the
> country, and in every case we've found
> an undercurrent of racial bias. That
> doesn't mean you hate black people, it
> merely means culturally speaking there
> is a predisposition for people to
> categorize those who are different.

                    THE SUSPECT
          So that's what you have to keep in
          mind. It is culture and attitude we're
          looking at, not right and wrong.
          Nobody's judging.

                    POLASKI SHERIFF
          I didn't do anything.

                    THE SUSPECT
          Which brings up our second point. Most
          times, folks don't have a good handle
          on how they come across.

                    POLASKI SHERIFF
          I'm not drunk, I know what I said.

As if to say, "really?" the Suspect un-pauses the tape.

                    POLASKI SHERIFF
                      (on TV)
          Polite time is over. You come to my
          town, take what's not yours, lie? I'll
          call you whatever I want, boy. And that
          ain't the worst of it.

Again, the Suspect hits the "PAUSE" button.

He looks to the sheriff, waiting patiently for a reaction. He has to wait awhile. Finally:

                    POLASKI SHERIFF
          It's all out of context.

                    THE SUSPECT
          We get that a lot, too. "Out of
          context." Actually, this experiment is
          specifically designed to contextualize
          these issues.

                    THE BANK ROBBER
                      (to the Suspect)
          Arthur, tell him about the
          Linguistics Department.

                    THE SUSPECT
          Back at the university, we have a team
          of language scientists who will parse
          the video.

                    POLASKI SHERIFF
          What does that mean, parse?

                     THE SUSPECT
Well, they go over it carefully.

                  THE BANK ROBBER
These are experts. For example, they'll be a column for "nigger," tracking the frequency of use --

                     THE SUSPECT
     (interrupting)
They factor in the volume, the vehemence of the usage, the repetition, that sort of thing.

                  THE BANK ROBBER
It's like threat assessment, or reading body language. What do people mean when they say "boy" a certain way.

                     THE SUSPECT
There's a lot of different ways to say that, all with different levels of malice.

                  THE BANK ROBBER
It's not just a matter of counting, either.

                     THE SUSPECT
Our lab will digitize the video and there are some pretty sophisticated computer programs to analyze them.

                  THE BANK ROBBER
Obviously, we'll need all your other interviews with me.
     (casual, to the Suspect)
I think they went through two tapes. Maybe three.

The sheriff looks sick.

                  POLASKI SHERIFF
It's all township property.

                     THE SUSPECT
Not a problem, we can make copies and return the originals.

> THE BANK ROBBER
> We have some forms in the car you'll
> need to sign.

> POLASKI SHERIFF
> I'm not letting you take these.

The Suspect and the Bank Robber catch each others' eyes.

> THE SUSPECT
> Just so we're clear, when we say no
> names will be part of the report, we
> mean people, towns, even states. That's
> a basic experimental principle we
> follow.

> THE BANK ROBBER
> We identify all this as simply a rural
> region in the Midwest.

> THE SUSPECT
> Midland could be anyplace.

> THE BANK ROBBER
> On the video, all faces will be
> pixillated, are you familiar with that
> concept?

> POLASKI SHERIFF
> Like on "Cops."

The sheriff has gone numb, moved to that place inside where fear slows the heart and softens the eyes' ability to focus.

> THE BANK ROBBER
> As will any identifying marks on your
> uniforms.

> POLASKI SHERIFF
> (repulsed)
> I don't care about the uniforms and the
> pixels. You do *not* have my permission
> to take this material.

> THE SUSPECT
> (in "sales" mode)
> Sir, we've had this conversation with
> law enforcement heads in a dozen other
> (MORE)

42.

THE SUSPECT (CONT'D)
communities and they all eventually
come around --

POLASKI SHERIFF
(interrupting)
Not this one. We are not racists.

THE SUSPECT
Either way, you have nothing to be
concerned about.

POLASKI SHERIFF
We are not racists here and we will not
have you paint us that way.

THE BANK ROBBER
We're not painting anybody any way.
This is a survey, you and your men are
data points.

The Polaski Sheriff is staring at the floor now, locked-in and determined like a child.

POLASKI SHERIFF
Our town is none of your business.

THE SUSPECT
We're tying to learn about the world,
sheriff. It's our job. Help us do it.
We helped you do your
job today.

POLASKI SHERIFF
Says you.

THE BANK ROBBER
A half hour ago you thought you had an
unsolved bank robbery on your hands.
That vanished.

THE SUSPECT
Now the worst part of your day is
wondering if you'll be represented as
some kind of a redneck in this
anonymous overhead transparency we
present next year at a conference a
thousand miles away.

POLASKI SHERIFF
That feels worse somehow.

                    THE BANK ROBBER
          The university's spent a bit of money
          to have us --

                    POLASKI SHERIFF
                 (interrupting)
          Not my problem.

                    THE SUSPECT
          No, but now that it's done, should all
          the work go to waste?

                    THE BANK ROBBER
          Can Arthur just add one thing? It may
          change your mind.
                 (to the Suspect)
          Tell him.

                    THE SUSPECT
          The check we've offered to cover the
          unplanned expenses you may have
          incurred? By endorsing it, the township
          grants us the rights to use the
          interview footage.

The Polaski Sheriff takes the cashier's check out from his shirt pocket.

                    POLASKI SHERIFF
          This?

He tears it in half. Lets the pieces fall to the floor.

                    POLASKI SHERIFF
          We don't need your money, we don't need
          to be crunched with your data, we don't
          need your experiment.

The Polaski Sheriff goes over to the entry door and swings it wide open.

                    POLASKI SHERIFF
          Get out of here.

                    THE SUSPECT
          They do experimentation in human
          sexuality. They get solid data on
          masturbation, cross-dressing, cheating.
          Do you think we'd ever know anything
          about that if people thought they'd
          personally --

                    POLASKI SHERIFF
                  (interrupting)
              I said get out of here.

The Suspect and the Bank Robber look at each other, upset.

                    THE BANK ROBBER
              Okay, we respect your decision.

                    THE SUSPECT
              But you are forcing us to repeat the
              experiment in a geographically adjacent
              area, so if we can at the very least
              count on your discretion in revealing
              our technique?

The Polaski Sheriff goes over to the video camera.

He ejects the cartridge, flips back the protective plastic guard and YANKS the magnetic tape out in long angry pulls, staring at the two strangers as he does.

                    POLASKI SHERIFF
              No one's talking about this, because
              none of it ever happened.

The Suspect and the Bank Robber slink past him.

INT. SILVER SEDAN //MOVING// -- EVENING

The Suspect drives. The Bank Robber looks over from the shotgun seat.

                    THE BANK ROBBER
              There was no chance he was even
              considering turning those tapes over
              for one second, was there?

                    THE SUSPECT
              Nope.

                    THE BANK ROBBER
              And he's going to be thinking about
              this all week.

                    THE SUSPECT
              All year, probably. The man just had to
              accept he's a goddamn racist. He's
              always been able to dance around it.
              Now he's looked into the mirror without
              a mask.

                    THE BANK ROBBER
          Kind of an unexpected benefit of doing
          this.

EXT. ROADSIDE NEAR TOWN LINE -- THAT MOMENT

The sedan passes a sign:

   "THANKS FOR VISITING POLASKI
    COME AGAIN"

INT. SILVER SEDAN //MOVING// -- BACK TO SCENE

                    THE BANK ROBBER
          What's it like, walking away with three
          hundred grand?

                    THE SUSPECT
          Feels pretty good. Maybe you'll see.
          Maybe you'll play the Bank Robber next
          time.
               (beat)
          And I'll try out Mr. Freeman Finch.

The Bank Robber starts laughing, and the Suspect can't help but join in...

INT. CELL, MIDLAND TOWNSHIP BUILDING -- DAY

Sheriff Dixon stares at the Suspect.

                    SHERIFF DIXON
          Freeman? Well? You have an answer? I
          asked you a question.

                    THE SUSPECT
          Am I going to admit the reason I'm
          here? I'll answer with a question. What
          the fuck's wrong with the explanation I
          already gave?

                    SHERIFF DIXON
               (scoffing)
          Looking at property?

                    THE SUSPECT
          You're concluding a man of my heritage
          can't buy land. Is that the crux of
          your case against me?

Dixon stands up, tired of waiting for a confession.

                    SHERIFF DIXON
          I'm going back over the video from the
          bank with a fine-toothed comb. You got
          anything to say to me, this is your
          last chance.

                    THE SUSPECT
          What would you want an innocent man to
          say, Gomer?

The sheriff shakes his head, boggled by the whole situation. He turns off the camcorder and leaves the cell.

EXT. BLUE-J MOTEL, RALEIGH -- DAY

The silver car is parked in front of the door to Room 107.

INT. BLUE-J MOTEL, ROOM 107 -- THAT MOMENT

The Bank Robber sits on one of the twin beds.

With a thumbnail, he carefully rifles the edge of the stack of currency. The PRINTED PAPER BAND around the stack reads:

     "CAROLINA CREDIT & TRUST
      U.S. TWENTY DOLLARS x 100"

INT. RECEPTION AREA, MIDLAND TOWNSHIP BUILDING -- DAY

Sheriff Dixon approaches Deputy Riley.

                    DEPUTY RILEY
          How'd it go?

                    SHERIFF DIXON
          Not great. How about you. Any luck with
          her?

They both eye Meredith, who sits quietly on a bench in the b.g. waiting to be allowed to leave.

                    DEPUTY RILEY
          She can't face him.

                    SHERIFF DIXON
               Yeah.

The sheriff looks around, thinking things out.

                    SHERIFF DIXON
               What would be great is for Meredith to
               say she saw the guy pull into the
               parking lot. Maybe saw his face as he
               got out, before he put the mask on.

                    DEPUTY RILEY
               Yeah, that'd be good.
                    (beat)
               Not the way it happened, though.

                    SHERIFF DIXON
                    (beat)
               Nope.

                    DEPUTY RILEY
               Nope.
                    (beat)
               If she won't ID him in person, I have
               another idea, though.

INT.   CELL, MIDLAND TOWNSHIP BUILDING -- DAY

The Suspect looks up as Deputy Riley unlocks the door and steps inside.

                    THE SUSPECT
               What's the situation?

Without a word, Riley moves in close and snaps a POLAROID PICTURE of the Suspect.

He's already walking away and locking the door as the instant photo whirs out of the camera's front.

                    THE SUSPECT
               Hey! What the hell is that for? I
               didn't give you...
                    (realizing Riley's gone)
               ...permission to do that.

EXT.   BLUE-J MOTEL, RALEIGH -- DAY

The Bank Robber comes out with the cardboard box in both hands and the duffle bag on top.

He's dressed in khakis and an oxford shirt. An ELECTRONIC MONEY COUNTER is wedged under his armpit.

He pops the trunk with the keychain remote. Drops the box and the money counter inside and slams the lid.

Moving around to the passenger side, he throws the duffle bag in. Then he climbs behind the wheel and starts the engine.

INT.   RECEPTION AREA, MIDLAND TOWNSHIP BUILDING-- EVENING

Heather stares at the Polaroid, trying to decide how to proceed. She looks around and notices a THICK PACKET OF PAPERS on the bulletin board.

The FBI's "Ten Most Wanted" list.

She takes it down and flips through it. Four of the ten are African-American men. She reaches for her scissors.

LATER --

TIGHT ON HEATHER'S DESK

as she cuts out the last of the four African-American FBI photos.

Including the cut-out Polaroid of the Suspect, there's a total of five pictures now.

Inspired, Heather picks up one of her glossy gossip magazines. She flips through the pages, looking for one more African-American.

She comes across a feature on Samuel L. Jackson and reaches for her X-Acto.

INT.   SILVER SEDAN //MOVING// -- EVENING

The Bank Robber drives along, psyching himself up.

                        THE BANK ROBBER
            (to himself)
You're smart, you're educated, you've got a doctorate in sociology, for Christ's sake.
            (beat)
You're a fucking pussy.

That concept makes him remember something. He pats down his pockets. Nothing. Then flips open the glove compartment. Still nothing.

                     THE BANK ROBBER
    Shit.

The Bank Robber's annoyed, but then sees something up ahead that gives him a little hope.

THROUGH THE WINDSHIELD

There's a GAS STATION/CONVENIENCE STORE off to the right.

EXT. GAS STATION -- MOMENTS LATER

The silver sedan pulls off the road.

It maneuvers into a parking spot directly across from the pump where a tough-looking PICKUP TRUCK DRIVER is gassing up his Ford.

The Bank Robber gets out of the car, nearly running into the Pickup Truck Driver.

                     PICKUP TRUCK DRIVER
    How's it going?

                     THE BANK ROBBER
    Not bad, thanks.

The Bank Robber locks his car with the remote control. It makes a sound the Pickup Truck Driver can't help but notice.

As the Bank Robber makes his way toward the convenience store, the Pickup Driver looks to his skanky FEMALE PASSENGER sitting in the truck.

                     PICKUP TRUCK DRIVER
    You see that? Does that Sambo think I'm
    gonna steal his piece-of-shit ride or
    something?

                     FEMALE PASSENGER
    You know what you oughta do? You should
    teach him a lesson.

As the door closes behind the Bank Robber, the Pickup Truck Driver digs a RUSTY SCREWDRIVER out of his truck bed.

He grips it like a knife.

INT.   GAS STATION CONVENIENCE STORE -- THAT MOMENT

The Bank Robber wanders between the aisles, looking lost.

The CASHIER, a stoner teenager, studies him carefully. A black man is something of a rarity in this store.

>   CASHIER
>   Help you, man?
>
>   THE BANK ROBBER
>   You have any reading glasses?
>
>   CASHIER
>   No, nothing like that.
>
>   THE BANK ROBBER
>   Okay. What about...
>   (thinking)
>   What about pipes?
>
>   CASHIER
>   You mean like... tobacco pipes?
>
>   THE BANK ROBBER
>   (a stupid idea)
>   Never mind.

EXT.   GAS STATION -- THAT MOMENT

The Pickup Truck Driver squats down next to the silver sedan's left rear tire. He JABS his screwdriver into the rubber.

Pulls it out, does it AGAIN.

INT.   GAS STATION CONVENIENCE STORE -- THAT MOMENT

>   CASHIER
>   We have a lost and found box.
>
>   THE BANK ROBBER
>   Are there any glasses in there?
>
>   CASHIER
>   Hold on.

The Cashier digs out the small cardboard box from under the counter and peers in.

>   CASHIER
>   Yeah.

                    THE BANK ROBBER
          Can I have them?

                    CASHIER
          Depends. You have to describe them so I
          know they're yours.

                    THE BANK ROBBER
          But they're not mine.

                    CASHIER
               (with a shrug)
          Says right on the box. "Claimant must
          describe item accurately."

Exasperated, the Bank Robber looks over the cigarette choices behind the Cashier. He puts a five on the counter.

                    THE BANK ROBBER
          Never mind. Just give me a pack of
          Viceroys.
               (then, taking a shot)
          They're plastic, two lenses, little
          hooks for behind your ears.

                    CASHIER
          Accurate enough for me.

He takes a pair of nerdy BLACK GLASSES out of the box and hands them to the Bank Robber.

EXT.   GAS STATION -- MOMENTS LATER

The Pickup Truck Driver is having trouble removing the screwdriver from the tire tread.

It's stuck up to the hilt.

                    FEMALE PASSENGER (O.S.)
               (hissing)
          He's coming back!

Finally with both hands and a foot on the wheel for leverage, the Pickup Truck Driver gets the screwdriver out, just as --

The Bank Robber comes between the two cars, tearing open the cellophane on his pack of smokes with his teeth. In his free hand, he works his remote control.

Beep-beep-chink -- all four doors unlock on command.

The Pickup Truck Driver steps between the Bank Robber and his silver sedan.

> PICKUP TRUCK DRIVER
> Hey slick, can I ask you something?
> What's with locking the doors? You
> don't trust your fellow man?

> THE BANK ROBBER
> You know what, man? Force of habit. I'm
> from the city.

> PICKUP TRUCK DRIVER
> That supposed to impress me?

The Bank Robber turns icy.

> THE BANK ROBBER
> I'm getting in my car now.

The Pickup Truck Driver takes the hint and steps aside.

> PICKUP TRUCK DRIVER
> Right. Have a nice evening, there.

The Bank Robber ignores him as he climbs into the car.

As the silver car pulls out of the station, the Pickup Truck Driver follows it with his eyes as it accelerates away.

> PICKUP TRUCK DRIVER
> Good luck. You're gonna need it.

INT.   RECEPTION AREA, MIDLAND TOWNSHIP BUILDING -- EVENING

Sheriff Dixon stands with Meredith. He holds up for her a hastily-made PHOTO ARRAY -- pictures of six African-Americans peek out through small squares cut in a manila folder.

> SHERIFF DIXON
> Do you recognize anyone you see here,
> Meredith? Take your time.

Meredith points to Samuel L. Jackson.

> MEREDITH
> That one, from the movies.

The sheriff tries to hide his frustration.

INT. SILVER SEDAN //MOVING// -- EVENING

The Bank Robber drives, trying to get his cigarette lit with the dashboard lighter.

The rear tire suddenly BLOWS. The steering wheel whips in the Bank Robber's hand. It has a mind of its own.

                    THE BANK ROBBER
      Fuck!

INT. RECEPTION AREA, MIDLAND TOWNSHIP BUILDING -- EVENING

Meredith pushed the photo array away from her.

                    MEREDITH
     Sheriff, I keep telling you I didn't
     see the man.

                    SHERIFF DIXON
     You know it was a man, don't you? See?
     There's things maybe you don't know you
     know.

EXT. FARM ROAD -- EVENING

The silver sedan fishtails across two lanes of empty pavement. It hits the shoulder hard, clipping a sign that reads:

   "BRIDGE FREEZES BEFORE ROAD"

The collision with the signpost swings the out-of-control car parallel to the road, and for a cruel instant it looks like it'll head straight onto the short bridge that spans a gorge.

Then the FRONT TIRE BLOWS. The sedan skids on the gravel and THUNDERS OFF A STEEP EMBANKMENT, just five yards from where the bridge's guardrail begins.

INT. RECEPTION AREA, MIDLAND TOWNSHIP BUILDING -- EVENING

Meredith looks at the photo array, flustered.

                    MEREDITH
     Do you think I can't tell what you did?
     Where these pictures came from? I'm not
     an idiot. Are you just trying to get me
     to say something that isn't true?

EXT. RAVINE -- EVENING

The silver sedan SCRAPES down the rocky face of the gorge almost vertically, kicking up SPARKS, taking out low vegetation and starting a small GRAVEL LANDSLIDE in its wake.

The undercarriage snags a loop of THICK TREE ROOT, which pulls out of the red clay dirt a few feet on both sides before holding its ground.

The silver sedan jerks to a stop, 40 mph to zero in a second.

The engine revs. The chassis creaks.

A wisp of exhaust comes out of the tailpipe.

The entire car is hanging nose-down by its rear axle in the shadow of the old bridge, fifteen feet below the road, and easily fifty above the ravine.

INT. SILVER SEDAN -- THAT MOMENT

The Bank Robber is a mess. Unconscious. With no seatbelt to hold him in place, his chest is taking the weight, pressed against the steering wheel.

He's been thrown headfirst into the windshield. It's spiderweb-cracked where his forehead made impact.

The lost-and-found glasses are sitting on the windshield as if they belong there.

The duffle bag has come to a rest in the foot well on the passenger side, along with the realistic toy gun.

SHADOWS CRAWL IN TIME-LAPSE as it gets later, darker.

The Bank Robber doesn't move.

EXT. MIDLAND TOWNSHIP BUILDING -- NIGHT

Heather approaches Sheriff Dixon, who stands staring out at the small town square, now lit.

He sees Meredith as well, looking at the same view he is. But she's outside, un-sheltered. Waiting rather than thinking.

>   HEATHER
> Sheriff? I'm going to take Meredith
> back to the bank. Her car's there.

                    SHERIFF DIXON
               (without looking at her)
          Okay.

                    HEATHER
          Then you want me to come back?

                    SHERIFF DIXON
          No, it's okay. You can go home.

                    HEATHER
          I don't mind.

Now Sheriff Dixon finally turns to face Heather.

                    SHERIFF DIXON
          What could you do here?

Heather can't see another opportunity to say her piece. She goes for it.

                    HEATHER
          What are you going to do with him?

                    SHERIFF DIXON
          I can hold him for forty-eight hours,
          Heather.

                    HEATHER
          I know, but... what's the charge? Being
          black?

                    SHERIFF DIXON
          How dare you?

                    HEATHER
          I'm sorry, but you taught me:
          I have to say something if I
          see injustice.

                    SHERIFF DIXON
          Is that what you see? You know me
          better than that.

                    HEATHER
          I thought I did. You don't have a
          witness, you don't have the money, you
          don't have a confession --

                    SHERIFF DIXON
               (interrupting)
          I have a feeling.

                    HEATHER
          I have a feeling too. I talked to him.
          He's not a thug.

                    SHERIFF DIXON
          People can fool you. You're just a kid,
          you don't get it yet. You never know
          what a man's capable of.

                    HEATHER
          Just promise me you'll think about what
          you're doing here. There's the right
          path and the wrong one. Make sure you
          know which you're on.

                    SHERIFF DIXON
          I'll give it all some thought. Now you
          make a promise for me. Take care of
          Meredith, get yourself home, and spend
          the evening trying to remember you
          don't really live in a town where
          things like this can happen.

Heather gives him a hopeful smile, picks up the keys from her desk and then she's out the door.

INT.   CELL, MIDLAND TOWNSHIP BUILDING -- EVENING

The sheriff walks in to find the Suspect squinting into the camcorder's viewfinder.

He tries a different tactic this time. Very casual, just two guys talking.

                    SHERIFF DIXON
          Tampering with evidence?

                    THE SUSPECT
          The clock on this thing set right?

                    SHERIFF DIXON
          Don't see why not. I'm not the
          technology whiz. You should see me
          trying to set my alarm.
                    (glancing at his watch)
          It's almost seven, if that's what
          you're asking.

                    THE SUSPECT
          That's what this says.

SHERIFF DIXON
Great. Everybody's in sync.

The Suspect wonders how to proceed. He's tense.

THE SUSPECT
Okay, something's obviously wrong.

SHERIFF DIXON
Besides the grand larceny, you mean?
'Cause that's about as wrong as it gets
around here.

For once the Suspect isn't interested in banter. He's trying to figure out how to approach the situation. Suddenly, it seems he's actually *feeling* the confinement of the cell.

THE SUSPECT
Something's not going according to
plan, so I guess I'm going to have to
make the presentation my colleague
usually makes.

ANGLE ON THE HALLWAY

Passing by, Deputy Riley stops in his tracks and looks over at the Suspect.

Something about his speech pattern, it's all wrong.

Like a *Mission: Impossible* mask has just been taken off, revealing someone entirely new.

DEPUTY RILEY
Did you say "colleague?"

IN THE CELL

Sheriff Dixon's interest is piqued as well. He talks to Riley with his eyes still locked on the Suspect.

SHERIFF DIXON
I'll handle this, deputy.

THE SUSPECT
I have to help you understand something
you're not going to want to process.
It'll take some getting used to.

SHERIFF DIXON
Is this a confession, Freeman?

                    THE SUSPECT
          Of a sort, but not the way you're
          thinking. I don't suppose we can go
          somewhere and talk?

                    SHERIFF DIXON
          Where do you believe we've been all
          day? This is a place to talk.

                    THE SUSPECT
          I don't think this cage is necessary
          anymore. Is there maybe an office we
          could use?

Dixon looks at the Suspect like he's crazy.

                    SHERIFF DIXON
          Nothing's changed. You're concerned
          it's 7:00, that's irrelevant to me --

                    THE SUSPECT
               (interrupting)
          It won't be.

                    SHERIFF DIXON
          -- and we're staying in this cell.

As the Suspect takes his seat Deputy Riley lets himself into the
cell. He goes over to the video camera to turn it on.

                    THE SUSPECT
          We don't need that anymore.

                    DEPUTY RILEY
          Like you say. We need to have
          a record.

                    SHERIFF DIXON
          Okay, Freeman, you've got everyone's
          attention. What's your big news?

                    THE SUSPECT
          There was no bank robbery.

The two policemen look at each other.

                    SHERIFF DIXON
          This your way of saying you're going to
          plead insanity?

                    THE SUSPECT
          It just looked like armed robbery.

SHERIFF DIXON
Is that right? Dead ringer, I'd say.

DEPUTY RILEY
(to the sheriff)
Yep, he's going for diminished capacity all right.

THE SUSPECT
Just listen. The man who... I don't want to say robbed the bank...

SHERIFF DIXON
Of course you don't.

THE SUSPECT
The man who <u>appears</u> to have robbed the bank, he wasn't me. He's my associate, and he should've brought the money back by now.

SHERIFF DIXON
Brought the money back.

THE SUSPECT
Something must have happened.

SHERIFF DIXON
I haven't dealt with a lot of armed felons, but that's not how they usually do things.

The Suspect's thinking, tamping down the panic.

THE SUSPECT
This is usually all wrapped up within a few hours.

DEPUTY RILEY
Usually?

THE SUSPECT
The biggest problem is the government. Did anybody call the FDIC yet?

SHERIFF DIXON
The what?

THE SUSPECT
Federal Deposit Insurance Corporation. They're the ones
who guarantee depositors' money. Has
(MORE)

                    THE SUSPECT (CONT'D)
          anyone from the bank reported the
          crime?

                    SHERIFF DIXON
          You'll get insight into how we're
          handling this investigation at your
          trial. Until then, that's proprietary
          information.

                    THE SUSPECT
               (furious)
          This whole goddamn --
               (catching himself, resetting)
          Please, I'm going to explain something
          that will make your life a hell of a
          lot easier than it's been today, I just
          need to know about the FDIC
          notification. We've done a couple of
          these where that call was made, and
          they screw everything up. Please.

                    SHERIFF DIXON
               (curiosity making him go
                along with it for now)
          I don't think anyone from the bank
          would call the government without
          clearing it with me.

                    THE SUSPECT
          Good, that's the big hurdle.

                    SHERIFF DIXON
          What's this all about?

The Suspect gets up, begins pacing the room.

                    THE SUSPECT
          I really don't know how this is going
          to go over, because traditionally when
          we discuss this, first off, my
          associate is in the room. That's
          important. But secondly, and more
          important psychologically, I think, is
          the money's already been returned.

                    SHERIFF DIXON
          You keep saying that. Which means,
          despite your earlier protests of
          innocence, you're involved in this.

                    THE SUSPECT
          I'm afraid you don't even know what
          "this" is, sheriff.

                    SHERIFF DIXON
          So why don't you go ahead and tell me
          what it is.

                    THE SUSPECT
          You're part of an experiment.

It's the last thing Sheriff Dixon and Deputy Riley would've ever expected to hear.

INT.   RECEPTION AREA, MIDLAND TOWNSHIP BUILDING -- LATER

Sheriff Dixon and Deputy Riley try to sort everything out.

                    DEPUTY RILEY
          That has got to be the craziest story I
          ever heard.

                    SHERIFF DIXON
          I know, part of me thinks the same
          thing. But another part is looking at
          the facts. You saw how concerned he was
          about the videotape always being on.
          All that talk about the way we say
          things...

                    DEPUTY RILEY
          Smoke and mirrors. He's got nothing
          else, he's down to diversionary
          tactics.

                    SHERIFF DIXON
          If he's the stick-up man, where's his
          car?

                    DEPUTY RILEY
          It broke down leaving the scene, so he
          stashed it in someone's barn.

                    SHERIFF DIXON
          And just started walking? The man stays
          on the main road, he doesn't keep to
          the woods.

                    DEPUTY RILEY
          There's all the ravines.

                    SHERIFF DIXON
          Which aren't much of a problem in the
          daylight, right? And where was he
          going? He was walking toward town.

                    DEPUTY RILEY
          He got turned around, that's all.

                    SHERIFF DIXON
          No, he was looking to get caught, he
          was looking like a criminal.

                    DEPUTY RILEY
          Because that's what he is.

                    SHERIFF DIXON
          Too much like one. There's something to
          this.

                    DEPUTY RILEY
          If you say so. But even if that's true,
          what are we supposed to do about it?

                    SHERIFF DIXON
          That's the question, Edgar. That's the
          magic question.

INT. CELL, MIDLAND TOWNSHIP BUILDING -- MOMENTS LATER

The sheriff and the deputy enter the cell. This time, they don't close the door behind them.

The Suspect stares at them, waiting for a reaction. They stare back.

                    THE SUSPECT
          You believe me?

                    SHERIFF DIXON
          You've given us an alternate theory of
          the crime --

                    THE SUSPECT
            (interrupting)
          I keep telling you it's not really a
          crime!

                    SHERIFF DIXON
          -- that has no more evidence than the
          theory we've been running with. Not
          only that, it's a convoluted puzzle
          box. Occam's razor tells us which one
                    (MORE)

SHERIFF DIXON (CONT'D)
we should pursue.
(off the Suspect's shock)
That's right, you know your Kafka, I know my English logicians. I keep saying, people can surprise you.

DEPUTY RILEY
So what we're stuck with is us needing some compelling evidence.

SHERIFF DIXON
We called the trooper barracks. They confirmed someone called Raleigh with a vague threat about a false crime somewhere in the state.

THE SUSPECT
We soft pedal. The experiment is crippled if a blanket warning goes out to banks statewide.

SHERIFF DIXON
State police considered it a prank and told the caller it was illegal.

DEPUTY RILEY
We tried the university. No one's there until Monday morning.

THE SUSPECT
We can't wait that long. Something happened to Arthur Greer. We have to find him now.

SHERIFF DIXON
The ball's in your court. Convince us, professor.

THE SUSPECT
The property I was looking at during the robbery, where I made it look like I could've buried money? I did bury something.

SHERIFF DIXON
What did you bury?

THE SUSPECT
It's my insurance policy. In case things go wrong. A fail safe.

                    SHERIFF DIXON
          Tell us what and where this fail safe
          is, we'll fetch it.

                    THE SUSPECT
               (shakes head vehemently)
          No, you'll never find it. I have to go
          with you.

The two lawmen regard each other, silently asking each other the same question. Is this a wild goose-chase?

EXT.   RURAL ROAD -- NIGHT

The headlights of the sheriff's slow-moving FOUR-WHEEL-DRIVE JEEP splash across a real estate sign:

   "FOR SALE -- FORECLOSURE BARGAIN
    22 ACRE COMMERCIAL FARM
    HOUSE + OUTBUILDINGS"

INT.   MIDLAND TOWNSHIP POLICE 4X4 //MOVING// -- NIGHT

Sheriff Dixon is behind the wheel, making his way carefully up the driveway.

                    THE SUSPECT (V.O.)
          It's just up here a ways.

IN THE BACKSEAT

behind the Plexiglas cage, Deputy Riley sits pressed up against the Suspect. The Suspect eyes the deputy's gun, the holster almost pressing against his thigh. He returns his attention to the view outside.

                    THE SUSPECT
          On your left. Before the barn.

The 4x4 slows down to a crawl.

EXT.   FORECLOSED PROPERTY -- NIGHT

The Suspect kneels in the fresh dirt, clawing at the earth with cuffed hands.

Above him, Riley and Dixon stare down, augmenting the glowing headlights of the police jeep with their own billy-club style flashlights.

Their holsters are unsnapped.

The Suspect has worked up a strip of earth a foot long and six inches deep.

                SHERIFF DIXON
      If the gun's stashed there, be
      forewarned. I'll ventilate you before
      you can raise it.

                THE SUSPECT
      There's no gun. The guy at the bank
      isn't the guy who was here.

The Suspect pulls a ZIP-LOC BAG out of the hole.

Inside, a BRASS KEY connected to a PLASTIC KEY FOB that reads:

  "BLUE-J MOTEL
   QUALITY WITHOUT THE COST"

                SHERIFF DIXON
      This is way over in Raleigh.

                THE SUSPECT
      The experiment requires that no one
      from the target town could possibly
      recognize us. You've got one bed and
      breakfast here.

                DEPUTY RILEY
        (to Sheriff Dixon)
      Word would get around.

Dixon holds the key in his flashlight beam, not impressed.

                SHERIFF DIXON
      This is your alibi.

INT. BLUE-J MOTEL, RECEPTION DESK -- NIGHT

The MOTEL RECEPTIONIST thinks hard, trying her best.

ANGLE ON THE REGISTRATION DESK

where the stamp-sized cut-out Polaroid of the Suspect sits.

              MOTEL RECEPTIONIST
      Yeah that him. I seen him. Number
      Twelve. Doctor Somebody.

                SHERIFF DIXON
      Dr. Finch?

MOTEL RECEPTIONIST
I don't remember his last name. He has a weird first name, though. All the girls in the coffee shop were talking about it. Freeman.

SHERIFF DIXON
Right... Did this Freeman sign a registration card or something along those lines?

MOTEL RECEPTIONIST
We take a credit card imprint.

The Motel Receptionist shuffles through papers and produces the right one. She looks at it closer, frowns.

MOTEL RECEPTIONIST
Oh. I forgot, the other one put his charge card down.

She hands the sheriff the sheet of paper. At the bottom, above a scrawled signature, it reads:

"ARTHUR M. GREER"

SHERIFF DIXON
They shared this one room?

MOTEL RECEPTIONIST
I know. They said they were on some kind of grant, and the budget was tight. I believe it must be, because honestly two rooms at the Blue-J won't exactly break the bank.

SHERIFF DIXON
I see you take down automobile information as well.

MOTEL RECEPTIONIST
People use our parking lot for the strip club across the street. Then guests don't have a spot...

SHERIFF DIXON
(reading)
Silver four-door, Illinois plates.

EXT. BLUE-JAY MOTEL PARKING LOT -- MOMENTS LATER

From the backseat of the sheriff's 4x4, The Suspect watches Sheriff Dixon and the Motel Receptionist walk from the office toward Room 107.

      THE SUSPECT
  Your boss is thorough, I'll give him
  that.

      DEPUTY RILEY
  What's Chicago like?

      THE SUSPECT
  Why? You aren't happy with Midland,
  Opie?

      DEPUTY RILEY
  I might like to see the world someday,
  that's all.

The Suspect looks this farm-raised man over.

      THE SUSPECT
  Yeah? Just goes to show you can't judge
  a book by its cover.

      DEPUTY RILEY
  You ever do this experiment with two
  white guys and a black town?

      THE SUSPECT
  Several times.

      DEPUTY RILEY
  Does it go the same way?

      THE SUSPECT
    (beat)
  Nope.

INT. BLUE-J MOTEL, ROOM 107 -- MOMENTS LATER

The fluorescent lights flicker on. Sheriff Dixon looks around, unsure what he hopes to find.

The Motel Receptionist hangs in the doorway.

      MOTEL RECEPTIONIST
  I'm supposed to be at the desk.

SHERIFF DIXON
               I'll just be a minute.

He looks under the twin beds. Nothing. In the closet. Nothing.
Room 107 is just an empty room. Except...

Sticking out from underneath one of the headboards, he finds a
WALLET-SIZE PHOTOGRAPH.

Dixon studies the picture for a clinical moment, then holds it
out to the Motel Receptionist.

                    SHERIFF DIXON
               You see anyone else with the men?

                    MOTEL RECEPTIONIST
               Nuh-uh.

The sheriff studies the photo for a moment. Then slips it in his
uniform's breast pocket and buttons the flap over it.

                    SHERIFF DIXON
               Does this phone still work if no one's
               booked in the room?

                    MOTEL RECEPTIONIST
               It's more trouble than it's worth to
               turn them off.

                    SHERIFF DIXON
               Do you suppose I could use it
               right quick?

INT.   BLUE-J MOTEL PARKING LOT -- LATER

Sheriff Dixon opens the back door of his 4x4 and looks across
his deputy to the Suspect.

                    SHERIFF DIXON
               Well, at least your buddy isn't dead in
               the motel room.

                    THE SUSPECT
               I could've told you that. Car's gone.

                    SHERIFF DIXON
               Your story checks out. To a point.

                    THE SUSPECT
               What exactly does that mean, to a
               point? It's all true! We did this last
               week in Minnesota. You call Orion
                         (MORE)

THE SUSPECT (CONT'D)
Savings & Loan there, they'll tell you the money was returned!

SHERIFF DIXON
That doesn't get you a pass. If we're not looking at armed robbery, there's still that whole slew of charges that could --

THE SUSPECT
(interrupting)
Do you honestly think the university would sign off on this research if we were exposed like that? If my associate had shown up, I'd be in that motel room by now, work done, no charges. I've seen it. This isn't a crime, it's a misunderstanding.

SHERIFF DIXON
It's more than that. Your story's compelling, but don't get cocky. Right now the only fact we can verify is, by your own admission you were a conspirator in an incident where a hell of a lot of money that's not yours has gone missing.

THE SUSPECT
We find my colleague, this will all get squared away.

SHERIFF DIXON
Did it ever occur to you that your "colleague" might've been tempted to keep what he took?

The Suspect takes a moment to play those variables out in his mind. We can see the calculations flicker in his cold eyes.

THE SUSPECT
No.

DEPUTY RILEY
That's what it's looking like.

THE SUSPECT
We are not criminals.

SHERIFF DIXON
Hey, you don't have to be a criminal to find yourself wanting to keep a huge sack of money you're suddenly holding.

DEPUTY RILEY
That's human nature.

THE SUSPECT
It's not like that. I know everything about him. It would be absolute suicide -- worse -- for him to do what you're suggesting.

SHERIFF DIXON
C'mon. You know money can buy a lot of privacy. Besides, knowing what a man did doesn't mean a whole lot if he's on some island with unusual extradition laws. He's got at least a day head start on you.

THE SUSPECT
It would've happened before.

The sheriff shrugs.

SHERIFF DIXON
Either way, the job's the same. We've got an APB out on the tags. Now he either went east on 37 toward the bank and something happened to him on the way or he went in any of a hundred other directions. If it's the first case we'll find him on the way back and hopefully it won't be too late. If it's the second, the state troopers will get him soon enough.

THE SUSPECT
He was coming to Midland. Trust me. Now maybe he was robbed, or in an accident, that's what concerns me. But no one's going to find him heading for the state line.

SHERIFF DIXON
I've gotta assume you're some mastermind of psychology. Is that how you can be so sure?

The Suspect considers this question.

INT. UNIVERSITY RESEARCH LAB -- DAY //FLASHBACK//

A FEMALE VOLUNTEER sits at a control panel that has several DIALS and a large RED BUTTON. There are serious-looking "HIGH VOLTAGE" warning stickers all over it.

An INSTRUCTOR sits at a desk outfitted with a gooseneck microphone. She reviews LARGE INDEX CARDS with printed words divided into four squares.

The Bank Robber stands behind the Instructor wearing a lab coat and clutching a clipboard. They're in the middle of a Stanley Milgram "conformity experiment."

SUPER OPTICAL: "TWO MONTHS EARLIER"

>   INSTRUCTOR
>   (into mic)
>   Fish and... A) chips, B) fowl,
>   C) bowl, or D) loaves.
>
>   TEST SUBJECT (O.S.)
>   (through speaker)
>   Oh... ah... I... I can't remember!
>
>   INSTRUCTOR
>   You must make a selection.
>
>   TEST SUBJECT (O.S.)
>   But it <u>hurts</u>. The last one stung bad,
>   and I can't concentrate.
>
>   INSTRUCTOR
>   A) chips, B) fowl, C) bowl, or D)
>   loaves. You've agreed to make a
>   selection.
>
>   TEST SUBJECT (O.S.)
>   I really don't want to...
>
>   INSTRUCTOR
>   The experiment requires that you make a
>   selection.
>
>   TEST SUBJECT (O.S.)
>   ...uh, okay. Give me... ah, D.
>
>   INSTRUCTOR
>   (to the Bank Robber)
>   That is an incorrect word pair.

                    THE BANK ROBBER
                  (to the FEMALE VOLUNTEER)
            Set your dial to 165 volts and then
            administer the punishment.

The girl doesn't budge. She stares at the curtain that separates
her from the Test Subject.

                    THE BANK ROBBER
            Miss Lerner? Turn your dial up to 165
            and continue, please.

                    FEMALE VOLUNTEER
            But it really sounded like it hurt the
            last time. He kind of yelped.

                    THE BANK ROBBER
            That's not your concern. He chose the
            wrong answer. You are obligated to
            continue.

A look to the Instructor. Blank-faced, no help there.

Finally, the student relents. She turns the dial, then presses a
button. A sharp electrical noise fills the room, and through the
speaker -- but also from behind that door -- the Test Subject
SHRIEKS.

Before the experiment can progress, the Suspect enters, dressed
in a sports coat and tie.

                    THE SUSPECT
                  (to the Bank Robber)
            I have to talk to you.

The Female Volunteer is looking for back-up, her moist eyes
searching the Suspect's steely ones.

                    FEMALE VOLUNTEER
                  (to the Suspect)
            Professor, I'm so glad you're here. Our
            test subject told us he has a heart
            condition!

                    THE SUSPECT
                  (rote, to the   Female
                   Volunteer)
            The experiment requires that you
            continue.
                  (to the Bank Robber)
            I really need you.

As he moves toward the door, the Bank Robber hands his clipboard to the Instructor.

                    THE BANK ROBBER
                      (to the Instructor)
            Up to five hundred volts.

As they exit, reveal behind the curtain, where the TEST SUBJECT merely pretends to be getting shocked.

INT. BASEMENT HALLWAY -- THAT MOMENT

The Suspect and Bank Robber step through a door marked:

   "GRADUATE PSYCH. DEPT.
    MEMORY TEST IN PROGRESS"

They make their way past TAs gathering and coordinating VOLUNTEERS for psychology experiments.

                    THE BANK ROBBER
            What's so urgent?

                    THE SUSPECT
            The whole thing. I'm telling you, it's
            down to a matter of weeks. Months,
            tops.

                    THE BANK ROBBER
            You're doing everything you can.

                    THE SUSPECT
            You know, starting right now, that's
            actually true for a change.

They arrive at the elevator.

                    THE BANK ROBBER
            Not the sixth floor. You know I don't
            have the stomach for actually seeing...
            I mean, it's bad enough thinking about --

                    THE SUSPECT
            Not six this time. I got to get out of
            this building. And you know what,
            brother? We're about to see exactly
            what you have the stomach for.

This answer the Bank Robber finds disturbing.

EXT. COLLEGE CAMPUS -- EVENING

The two men cross the university's quad, in front of the squat and Gothic HALL OF LANGUAGES.

>   THE BANK ROBBER
> Right on, man. A little fresh air. Do
> you good. You spend too much time in
> that place.

The Suspect's eyes are fixed dead ahead, determined.

>   THE SUSPECT
> Time is a hell of a precious resource.

>   THE BANK ROBBER
> So, something changed on six?

>   THE SUSPECT
> What makes you so sure this is about
> her?

>   THE BANK ROBBER
> Come on.

>   THE SUSPECT
> Couldn't it be...

But the Suspect can't even think of an alternative.

>   THE BANK ROBBER
> Yeah, of course. Acid rain, the grassy
> knoll, the 1919 White Sox. This is
> about the situation because it's always
> about the situation, so the situation
> must've gotten worse.

>   THE SUSPECT
> Worse? How can it?
>   (beat)
> Nothing's changed on six.

>   THE BANK ROBBER
> Why'd you pull me away in the middle of
> the experiment, then?

                    THE SUSPECT
          Nothing's changed with her. But me?
          Something did. I saw the light. I now
          realize action is required. Action is
          everything.

                    THE BANK ROBBER
          I don't like where this is going. The
          list --

                    THE SUSPECT
                (interrupting)
          The list is false hope.

                    THE BANK ROBBER
          It's the process.

                    THE SUSPECT
          It's lighting a fucking candle on the
          altar. Waiting won't work. Those people
          aren't going to do anything about it.
          So we are.

                    THE BANK ROBBER
          We?

INT. GARAGE -- NIGHT

Half workshop, half storage room.

The Suspect and The Bank Robber sit on two VINYL BENCH SEATS long-ago yanked like teeth from some junker school bus.

A SLIDE PROJECTOR sits between them, set up on a chessboard.

The Suspect grabs two glasses and fills them with healthy pours of vodka.

The Suspect grabs the slide projector's "remote control," a box attached by a long cord. The light blares directly out, flaring into the camera lens. We see nothing.

                    THE SUSPECT
          Tell me the truth. Is that anyone you
          recognize? I need you to see what I
          see.

Stunned, the Bank Robber looks like he's going to pass out.

>THE BANK ROBBER
>I feel for you, man. It's no cakewalk for me to live through this, either. But this here's bush-league psychology. That doesn't work on professionals.

Undeterred, the Suspect flicks through the slides.

>THE SUSPECT
>We'll see. I need you to understand that we can't live on hope anymore.

>THE BANK ROBBER
>And man, what is there but hope at this point?

The Suspect gathers his nerve. Never said it out loud before.

>THE SUSPECT
>The black market.

>THE BANK ROBBER
>Sure, the black market. Right. The whole gang on-board with that?

>THE SUSPECT
>It's a unilateral decision.

>THE BANK ROBBER
>That's not a plan. For starters, you don't even know how to find --

>THE SUSPECT
>(interrupting)
>There are ways. Believe it or not, even the people involved purely on a professional level, the ones with no skin in the game? Some hate the way it goes, hate the red tape. Someone on the sixth floor gave me a lead. It's in Argentina.

>THE BANK ROBBER
>This isn't something you buy your way out of.

>THE SUSPECT
>If you have to it is, man, and it isn't bargain basement. You pay and you pay. But you know I can't let a
>(MORE)

                    THE SUSPECT (CONT'D)
          thing like that constrain
          my options.

                    THE BANK ROBBER
          I don't know a lot about the black
          market, but...

                    THE SUSPECT
          Well, it doesn't take credit cards.

                    THE BANK ROBBER
          You'd have to rob a bank to get the
          kind of money you'd need.

He's joking, but the Suspect smiles in a way that has nothing to
do with humor.

                    THE SUSPECT
          You get caught robbing a bank. I don't
          intend on going to prison.
               (beat)
          But I've been looking into it. There
          are alternatives.

                    THE BANK ROBBER
          That's crazy. You're not a criminal.

                    THE SUSPECT
          No, I'm not, but I've figured a way to
          make it rain money, which is critical
          right now. No one knows they've been
          taken off. I've looked at it from every
          angle.

                    THE BANK ROBBER
          Except the one that helps you see
          you're risking your life.

                    THE SUSPECT
          Bottom line, this needs to happen. And
          if I can't do it, what the fuck's my
          life worth anyway?

The Bank Robber has no comeback to that.

                    THE BANK ROBBER
          We're family. I got your back. So
          what's the move?

                    THE SUSPECT
          You and I are going on sabbatical.
          There's this place I've discovered, a
                         (MORE)

                    THE SUSPECT (CONT'D)
          place of higher learning in a certain
          artistic field of endeavor.

                    THE BANK ROBBER
          Where?

                    THE SUSPECT
          The Bronx.

INT. PRINTING PLANT MACHINE ROOM -- DAY

[Dialogue bleeds in from previous scene]

The Suspect and the Bank Robber try to talk with THE
COUNTERFEITER -- a wiry force of nature, part mad scientist.

In the b.g., a gigantic industrial WEB-FED PRESS operates with
clanging ferocity, pumping out a stream of paper CRISS-CROSSED
WITH DOZENS OF GREEN CURRENCY-SIZED IMAGES.

GRUNGY MEN work the sheets over with PRECISION PAPER CUTTERS.

                    THE COUNTERFEITER
          Staten Island says you told him you
          think you can move amounts in the
          hundreds of thousands.

                    THE SUSPECT
          If you can make it, we can move it.

The Counterfeiter is annoyed and maybe even slightly suspicious.
He turns away.

                    THE COUNTERFEITER
          I always knew Staten Island was an
          idiot. You're wasting my fucking time.
          I'm an artist, and you know artists are
          touchy fucks. So if I were you, I'd
          leave before you get on my bad side.

The Suspect and the Bank Robber share a look. The Bank Robber
urges the Suspect on with his eyes: Come on, go for it.

                    THE SUSPECT
          We can get three hundred grand into
          circulation in one day. Maybe more.
          Just give us a shot.

                    THE COUNTERFEITER
                  (over his shoulder)
               Give us... You fuck-ups know anything
               about laundering money?

                    THE BANK ROBBER
               We have a plan.

The word "plan" rubs the Counterfeiter wrong. It's clarification
time, time for a lecture he's clearly given often in the past.

                    THE COUNTERFEITER
               I'll bet you do. Couple of cowboys, got
               it all figured out. Do you know every
               shithead lowlife in America would be
               faking money if they could get their
               greasy hands on a thirty million-dollar
               Reichenbach web-fed press. But they
               don't have two dimes to rub together
               and I was smart enough to procure one,
               so they gotta come to me with their
               stupid ideas.

                    THE SUSPECT
               That's the thing, your expenses are
               fixed. How much can it cost you to
               print three hundred K for us? A
               thousand bucks?

                    THE BANK ROBBER
               If that.

                    THE SUSPECT
               I may not be in your line of work, but
               I've got enough sense to know your
               issue isn't a matter of production.
               What you have is a distribution
               problem.

Now the Suspect has the Counterfeiter's undivided attention.

INT.   COUNTERFEITER'S OFFICE -- MOMENTS LATER

                    THE SUSPECT
               Say we leave here with that kind of
               cash and get shot down like dogs, what
               are you really out?

                    THE COUNTERFEITER
Oh, I'm out all right, gents. You'll leave a little blood trail right to my door, is all.

                    THE SUSPECT
Check me out. Do I really look like the kind of man who's planning on getting himself killed?

                    THE COUNTERFEITER
Anybody who tells me they got a way to move that much questionable paper in one throw is deluded. So it don't much matter if you _seem_ like you got a death wish. 'Cause I hate to break it to you, but you _do_ got a death wish.

                    THE SUSPECT
Maybe. But flip it around. We take three hundred in bad paper, show up back here in less than a week, slap down a clean hundred grand, that's what? A thousand-fold return on your manufacturing costs. How's that sound to you?

                    THE COUNTERFEITER
Like a crack-pipe dream.

                    THE SUSPECT
We got an angle. And we're talking no-risk to you.

                    THE COUNTERFEITER
No-risk. Well, like I said homies, nada such thing as no-risk when I let my bills out that door.

The Suspect shakes his head at the Bank Robber. No sale.

They both start toward the door. The moment before they're out of the Counterfeiter's life forever, he reconsiders.

                    THE COUNTERFEITER
Hold up!

The two criminals freeze in the doorway.

                    THE COUNTERFEITER
What do you drive?

                    THE BANK ROBBER
                  (confused)
          How's that?

                    THE COUNTERFEITER
                  (as if they're retarded)
          What kind of motor vehicles do you
          bullnuts drive?

                    THE SUSPECT
          Nissan Altima.

                    THE BANK ROBBER
          An SUV.

                    THE COUNTERFEITER
          An SUV? My work requires the kind of
          specificity you can't begin to
          appreciate. Let's try again.

                    THE BANK ROBBER
          It's a Stout Scarab, okay?

                    THE COUNTERFEITER
          They still making those pieces of crap?
                  (beat)
          Okay. Three hundred dirty on loan. You
          owe me a century clean. And I'll hold
          onto both your pink slips for
          collateral.

INT. PRINTING PLANT MACHINE ROOM -- LATER

The Counterfeiter comes over to them lugging a CARDBOARD BOX. It's filled with CASH.

The Bank Robber takes the box. The Suspect takes a quick glance over his partner's shoulder to see what's inside.

                    THE SUSPECT
          This is great, man. You won't regret
          it. Only thing, though...

                    THE COUNTERFEITER
                  (to himself)
          Here we go...

                    THE SUSPECT
          No, it's just... It's all fifties. We
          can't put all these fifties to work. We
          need every denomination.

                    THE COUNTERFEITER
              (with a frustrated sigh)
          Your plan, huh?

Annoyed with himself for getting talked into this, he takes the
box back and starts switching out the piles of bills.

*[Following scenes are a compressed version of previous robbery
flashback from pgs. 23-42. New angles reveal the existence of
counterfeit money in addition to the stolen "bank" money.]*

EXT. NORTHSTAR MOTEL, ST. PAUL -- MORNING

The Bank Robber and the Suspect speak with a Maid.

                    THE SUSPECT
          Hey. Do you know where Polaski is?

EXT. FARM ROAD, POLASKI -- DAY

The silver sedan is on the shoulder by a REAL ESTATE SIGN.

The Suspect and the Bank Robber talk through the driver's side
window.

                    THE SUSPECT
          You ready?

                    THE BANK ROBBER
          Ready as I'll ever be.

EXT. ORION SAVINGS & LOAN, POLASKI -- DAY

The Suspect gets out of the silver car with an EMPTY DUFFLE BAG.

He looks around nervously, then heads toward the door as he
fishes a SKI MASK out of his jacket pocket.

INT. ORION SAVINGS & LOAN, POLASKI -- MOMENTS LATER

Robbery in progress. Cash getting stuffed into the duffle bag.

                    THE SUSPECT (O.S.)
          Let's go! Come on!

EXT. FARM ROAD -- DAY

The Bank Robber shuffles along the side of the road.

Two Polaski Patrol Cops climb out of their cruiser.

> FIRST PATROL COP
> Sir! Stop your walking and turn around right now!

INT. NORTHSTAR MOTEL ROOM -- DAY

The Suspect stands between twin beds, on the phone.

> OPERATOR (V.O.)
> (through phone)
> Dr. Greer? This is the four o'clock reminder call you asked for.

> THE SUSPECT
> (into phone)
> Yeah, thank you.

On the left bed, the duffle bag sits with the bank's money spilled out. On the right one the Counterfeiter's cardboard box filled with counterfeit currency.

The Suspect returns to the electronic money counter on the desk. While the machine counts the fake money into neat stacks, the Suspect removes the bands on the real currency -- they have all the denominations on them, and each one reads:

"ORION SAVING & LOAN"

With assembly-line rhythm, the Suspect re-bands the counterfeit bills with the bank's paper bands.

He stacks them next to the duffle bag, putting the bank's stack on the bed next to the cardboard box.

INT. POLASKI GOVERNMENT CENTER -- DAY

The Bank Robber sits chained to the Sheriff's desk. A CAMCORDER is running in the corner, set up on a tripod.

> THE BANK ROBBER
> Why do you keep saying "boy?"

                    POLASKI SHERIFF
          I'm not calling you "boy," that's in
          your head.

EXT. NORTHSTAR MOTEL, ST. PAUL -- DAY

The Suspect puts the cardboard box of currency in the silver sedan's trunk, along with the money counting machine.

He opens the driver's side, carefully pushing the duffle bag in ahead of him, across the bench seat to the passenger side. Then the Suspect gets behind the wheel.

EXT. ORION SAVINGS & LOAN PARKING LOT, POLASKI -- LATER

The cops surround the Suspect, all pointing their guns. The Suspect is flat on the pavement, the duffle bag out of reach.

                    THE SUSPECT
          I'm not armed.

                    FIRST COP
                (to the other cops)
          Holy geez. That's the duffle bag from
          the security tape.

The First Cop kicks the bag, feels the give.

                    SECOND COP
                (to the Suspect)
          What's in there?

                    FIRST COP
          Johnny? This is... Christ, this is the
          money from the robbery.

INT. ORION SAVINGS & LOAN, POLASKI -- LATER

                    THE SUSPECT (O.S.)
          I can explain everything.

TIGHT ON THE DESK

There are two different KERSANDS UNIVERSITY BUSINESS CARDS, A GUN, and a CASHIER'S CHECK.

The Polaski Sheriff picks up the business cards.

                    POLASKI SHERIFF
                        (reading)
                "Arthur Greer, PhD."

                    THE SUSPECT
                That's me.

                    POLASKI SHERIFF
                        (reading)
                "School of Social Sciences."

                    THE SUSPECT
                Specifically, the Department of Social
                Psychology. And of course you already
                know my associate, Freeman Finch.
                Freeman's with the African-American
                Studies program.

The Bank Robber holds out his cuffed hands to shake.

The sheriff stares him down.

                    THE SUSPECT
                Ladies and gentlemen, we'd like to
                share some news with you. You're all
                part of an unique experiment in racial
                dynamics and bias.

The Bank Manager comes over from behind the teller counter.

                    BANK MANAGER
                It's all here. Every dollar.

INT. POLASKI GOVERNMENT CENTER -- DAY

The Polaski Sheriff goes over to the video camera.

He ejects the cartridge, flips back the protective plastic guard and YANKS the magnetic tape out in long angry pulls, staring at the Suspect and the Bank Robber as he does.

                    POLASKI SHERIFF
                No one's talking about this, because
                none of it ever happened.

INT. SILVER SEDAN //MOVING// -- DAY

The Suspect drives, the Bank Robber rides shotgun.

                    THE SUSPECT
          The man just had to accept he's a
          goddamn racist. He's always been able to
          dance around it. Now he's looked into
          the mirror without a mask.

                    THE BANK ROBBER
          Kind of an unexpected benefit of doing
          this.

EXT. ROADSIDE NEAR TOWN LINE -- THAT MOMENT

The sedan passes a sign:

   "THANKS FOR VISITING POLASKI
    COME AGAIN"

INT. SILVER SEDAN //MOVING// -- BACK TO SCENE

                    THE BANK ROBBER
          What's it like, walking away with three
          hundred grand?

                    THE SUSPECT
          Feels pretty good. Maybe you'll see.
          Maybe you'll play the Bank Robber next
          time.
                 (beat)
          And I'll try out Mr. Freeman Finch.

The Bank Robber and the Suspect starts laughing, but after a moment, it dies down.

                    THE BANK ROBBER
          Can I see it?

                    THE SUSPECT
          I suppose we've got enough tar between
          us now.

The Suspect pulls over on the shoulder.

EXT. ROADSIDE PAST TOWN LINE -- MOMENTS LATER

The Bank Robber and the Suspect stand by the rear of the car.

The Suspect pops the trunk with the remote.

The two men stare down at the money counter and the cardboard box filled with the bank's clean, untraceable cash.

They've just laundered more than a quarter of a million counterfeit dollars in one afternoon.

Slowly, the smiles leak out.

                    THE SUSPECT
        Psychology's a hell of a thing.

EXT. PRINTING PLANT, THE BRONX -- NIGHT

The Counterfeiter looks at the LIVE VIDEO FEED of --

The Suspect stands on the building's stoop, staring right into the camera. He holds a BULGING BRIEFCASE.

                THE COUNTERFEITER (V.O.)
           (through intercom, filtered)
        You sure you weren't followed?

The Suspect presses the "TALK" button as he looks around casually.

                    THE SUSPECT
        Don't see why I would be. I haven't
        done anything wrong.

The Counterfeiter presses the entry buzzer and watches the Suspect enter on his screen.

INT. PRINTING PLANT OFFICE -- MOMENTS LATER

The Suspect opens the briefcase on a desk.

                    THE SUSPECT
        As promised, your cut. A hundred grand.
        Clean as a baby's ass.

                THE COUNTERFEITER
        I don't know what kind of babies you've
        been hanging out with...

The Counterfeiter takes out a bill, feels it, holds it up to the light, murmuring in satisfaction all the while.

And finally, the most critical inspection, he takes out a JEWELER'S LOUPE and examines it closely.

                    THE COUNTERFEITER
          I guess maybe Staten Island isn't as
          stupid as he's always seemed. Okay, so
          we don't need this...

The Counterfeiter steps over to a smudged BULLETIN BOARD.

He takes down a sheet of paper, folds it several times, and tears it up.

                    THE SUSPECT
          What was that?

                    THE COUNTERFEITER
          Oh, I'm gonna call it a kind of
          insurance policy on the deal.

                    THE SUSPECT
          You have our pink slips.

                    THE COUNTERFEITER
          Those were to protect my investment.
          This...
               (points to the shredder)
          ...is to protect my reputation. If you
          didn't make good, I was going to have
          you killed.

                    THE SUSPECT
               (unimpressed)
          Ah. Always have to have a Plan B.

                    THE COUNTERFEITER
          Something tells me I'm preaching to the
          choir on that. You seem like a man who
          prepares for contingencies. Take your
          friend, who's suddenly MIA? Maybe around
          the corner so if you don't come back in
          ten you have some leverage? That your
          Plan B?

                    THE SUSPECT
          Let's say... whenever you start a new
          venture, I believe it's wise to make
          sure you're covered.

The Counterfeiter hands him two car registration slips. He looks at the hundred grand again.

                    THE COUNTERFEITER
          How did you do it?

                    THE SUSPECT
               Trade secret.

                    THE COUNTERFEITER
               Trade...? Nah. In my business the past
               is motherfucking prologue.

The Counterfeiter draws cold steel, jams it under the
Suspect's jaw.

                    THE COUNTERFEITER
               Answer me!

The Suspect remains quiet.

Bluff called, the Counterfeiter's up against it now. He backs
down, taking the tension off the pistol's hammer.

                    THE COUNTERFEITER
               The hell with the past, I can live with
               that. I don't stick my nose where it
               doesn't belong. Let's focus on the
               future of this relationship. So read me
               some fucking tea leaves.

                    THE SUSPECT
               The future is you give us four hundred
               thousand this time, you get a hundred
               in return.

                    THE COUNTERFEITER
               Staten Island really should've told you
               I don't cotton to pay cuts.

                    THE SUSPECT
               One-third was the introductory offer.
               Now that you know we can walk the walk,
               it's time to get down to brass bullets.
               Twenty-five percent off no-risk is a
               good set-up for you and you know it.

The Counterfeiter weighs the options, looks at the briefcase of
currency. The stranger is right, this is an offer he'd be crazy
to refuse.

                    THE COUNTERFEITER
               Done.

                    THE SUSPECT
               And in the spirit of full disclosure,
               you should know this is the last time
               we're ever doing this dance.

The Counterfeiter offers a knowing smile.

> THE COUNTERFEITER
> I've heard a lot of people say that. They try to move a little paper to pay off a debt, swear it won't get under their skin. Greed has a way of getting, though. Time'll tell. I'm betting I see your ass around here.

He opens the office door and shouts outside.

> THE COUNTERFEITER
> Rocco! Find me a big fucking cardboard box!

INT. MIDLAND TOWNSHIP POLICE 4X4 //PARKED// -- NIGHT

The Suspect stares at Sheriff Dixon.

> THE SUSPECT
> I'm one hundred percent sure Dr. Greer didn't take off with the money and leave me.

> SHERIFF DIXON
> (to Riley)
> Must be up for tenure.

> THE SUSPECT
> You ever play chess?

> SHERIFF DIXON
> All the time.

> THE SUSPECT
> You know how when you get to know how someone else plays their game, and they learn yours, it's almost always a stalemate?

> SHERIFF DIXON
> Yeah.

> THE SUSPECT
> But you know how you'd rather play that person than play someone else you might beat. There's a comfort there, even in the futility? That's how I know my man didn't make a border run with the money.

Dixon considers that for a moment. Then he taps on Riley's shoulder, motioning the deputy to get out of the jeep.

EXT.   BLUE-J MOTEL PARKING LOT -- THAT MOMENT

Riley gets out, leaving the Suspect inside.

> DEPUTY RILEY
> What's it look like?

Sheriff Dixon looks around, as if reticent to say it aloud.

> SHERIFF DIXON
> My gut tells me this actually played out the way Sigmund Freud here says it did. His friend has the money, he was on his way to return it, and now he and the money are at the bottom of one of these godforsaken ravines.

> DEPUTY RILEY
> So do we call out the volunteers, start organizing search parties?

EXT.   BLUE-J MOTEL PARKING LOT -- THAT MOMENT

The Suspect watches from the sheriff's 4x4 as the sheriff and the deputy talk low and close, looking in toward him occasionally.

The sense of paranoia is overwhelming. After taking all he can, the Suspect begins to relieve the pressure by singing:

> THE SUSPECT
> *There's a blackbird sitting on yonder hedge/He'll sing for you til you forget/Then he'll fly away, come back another day/There's a blackbird sitting on your window ledge/But don't you cry, don't you fret/He'll fly away, come back another day/Bah bah bah bah ba da da, da na na na na na.*

EXT.   BLUE-J MOTEL PARKING LOT -- THAT MOMENT

The two lawmen continue to strategize.

> SHERIFF DIXON
> I'm inclined to see where it leads without involving the cavalry. Now you don't have to --

                    DEPUTY RILEY
                  (interrupting)
              No. I'd want to be a part of that.

                    SHERIFF DIXON
              We just have to be aware of the
              dangers. The risk we're taking on. It's
              not the kind of risk you agreed to when
              you took the job.

                    DEPUTY RILEY
              Like you said, see where it leads.

                    SHERIFF DIXON
              Nothing like this has ever come along
              in our town. I just need to know where
              you stand, and know that if things go
              down suddenly, we're on the same page.

                    DEPUTY RILEY
              Definitely.

                    SHERIFF DIXON
              Okay, then.

They both put their hats on and turn back to the 4x4.

EXT.   GAS STATION -- NIGHT

The sheriff's 4x4 glides slowly past the place where the Bank Robber replaced his prop glasses.

On the opposite side of the road, there is only dark growth. The side-mounted spotlight on the sheriff's car skips over it, trying in vane to penetrate.

Bits of the green canopy are illuminated for a heartbeat, then fade into the blackness.

INT.   MIDLAND TOWNSHIP POLICE 4X4 //MOVING// -- LATER

The sheriff works the side-mounted spot with a control handle where the wing vent window used to be.

                    SHERIFF DIXON
                  (to the Suspect)
              Why'd you pick our town? We're not
              racists here.

> THE SUSPECT
> That's two different questions. The way we pick our sites, it's all demographics. We don't sit down and say, "Let's expose those backwards people in Midland." It's about distance from airports and colleges, whether there's a daily newspaper. It's a reliable formula.

> SHERIFF DIXON
> That doesn't make me feel a whole lot better.

> THE SUSPECT
> The answer to your second question is you are racist. You always are. You are not the exception, there _are_ no exceptions.

> DEPUTY RILEY
> Sheriff, right there!

Deputy Riley points out the window on his side.

RILEY'S POV

The spotlight picks up a banged-up sign:

"BRIDGE FREEZES BEFORE ROAD"

> SHERIFF DIXON
> Wasn't like that yesterday.

> DEPUTY RILEY
> No sir.

The sheriff pulls the 4x4 onto the shoulder.

EXT. COUNTY ROAD -- THAT MOMENT

All three men get out of the 4x4.

If the two lawmen remember they have a prisoner, they don't seem to care. They're transfixed by the BURNED TIRE TRACKS that run from the sign straight over the embankment.

They follow the tracks to the ridge's edge with their flashlights first, and when the road's shoulder falls away into pitch black, they physically move over to the --

EXT. RAVINE -- THAT MOMENT

They stare down at the silver sedan.

It's perpendicular to them, facing straight down. The red taillights and orange Illinois license plate reflect their flashlight beams.

> SHERIFF DIXON
> That your friend?

The Suspect is stunned. It's as if his car has been caught in a giant spider web.

> THE SUSPECT
> Yeah.

> SHERIFF DIXON
> That's good news. He was coming back after all.

> THE SUSPECT
> I told you.

> DEPUTY RILEY
> You think he survived that?

> SHERIFF DIXON
> Only one way to tell, Edgar. So who's going down?

> THE SUSPECT
> Me.

Both lawmen look at the Suspect.

> SHERIFF DIXON
> I don't think so.

> THE SUSPECT
> Are you kidding, man? Look at you...
>   (to Riley)
> And look at you. Laurel and Hardy. If he's hurt, neither of you have the muscle to pull him up.

> SHERIFF DIXON
>   (getting talked into it)
> Well, you did create this mess. And he _is_ your boy. Oh. Can I use that word? Is that okay under these circumstances?

                    DEPUTY RILEY
          We're the police, sheriff, this here is
          our job.

                    SHERIFF DIXON
          Our jobs were pretty quiet until
          Freeman got to town.

The Suspect can see it in Dixon's eyes, though. The deputy will
get nowhere. It's a *fait accompli*.

                    SHERIFF DIXON
          If he really wants to make the case
          that his little stunt at our bank was
          high-minded science and not a crime,
          why should we have to risk our life and
          retrieve your witness?

Dixon turns to the Suspect.

                    SHERIFF DIXON
          We've wasted enough of our energy. Go
          fetch your credentials, professor. That
          check from the university you were
          talking about. And all that
          misunderstood money. I'll get an
          ambulance out here for your friend.

LATER --

TIGHT ON THE SUSPECTS HANDS

as the handcuff key releases them.

The Suspect takes the cuffs and clips both bracelets around his
belt, making a small metal loop out of the short chain between
the two.

TIGHT ON THE JEEP'S FRONT BUMPER

as Deputy Riley unwinds a length of the METAL WINCH ROPE.

TIGHT ON THE SUSPECTS BELT

as the fat WINCH HOOK slides into the handcuff chain.

ANGLE ON THE RAVINE EDGE

The winch rope is taut. The Suspect backed to the edge of the
drop, connected to the jeep. He's gripping the big flashlight.

                              THE SUSPECT
                    You're absolutely sure you put the
                    parking brake on?

                              DEPUTY RILEY
                    Don't worry.

Riley moves a lever by the winch drum, and with a mechanical hum
the line slowly lets out.

The Suspect goes o v e r the edge.

He works his way slowly toward the car, his flashlight only
showing him how little there is to hold onto. Gnarled vines and
a few saplings.

He hears the engine, still running. A low, hurt rumble.

His beam catches the root that's holding the sedan in place. It
sends a chill down his spine.

Soon he's next to the passenger side door. He lets himself pass
it, working on a strategy.

When he's alongside of the hood, the Suspect finds a foothold on
the flattened front tire. The sedan creaks with his weight, but
stays in place.

                              THE SUSPECT
                         (calling up)
                    Hold up! I got it!

The winch stops smoothly. Now the Suspect has some slack. He's
able to reach up along the fender and get a hold of the door
handle.

The door POPS open over his head, coming straight out from the
body of the car like an old-fashioned ironing board.

The interior dome light comes on, illuminating the Bank Robber's
bloody face, pressed against the cracked windshield.

                              THE SUSPECT
                    Jesus.

The Suspect throws his glowing flashlight onto the surface of
the open door.

Then he pulls himself onto the door and climbs inside the front
seat, pulling the three feet of slack winch cable in with him.

INT. SILVER SEDAN -- THAT MOMENT

The "door open" buzzer seems as loud as a missile attack.

The Suspect scrambles into the front seat and crawls across the dashboard on hands and knees to get to the Bank Robber.

He checks the driver's pulse with one hand, while reaching around the steering column and turns the ignition off with the other.

>   THE SUSPECT
>   Wesley? Oh, c'mon.

But it's a lost cause. The Bank Robber is dead.

EXT. SILVER SEDAN -- MOMENTS LATER

The Suspect points his flashlight straight up, waving it. He's standing up unsteadily, like he's on a diving board.

>   THE SUSPECT
>   (calling up)
>   Hey! He's dead! Can you hear me?

EXT. RAVINE'S EDGE -- THAT MOMENT

The sheriff and his deputy look down at the Suspect. Dixon is now smoking a CIGAR.

>   SHERIFF DIXON
>   (calling down)
>   We can hear you. Your science is pretty
>   dangerous, eh professor? It killed a
>   man.

>   THE SUSPECT (O.S.)
>   (faint)
>   What should I do?

>   SHERIFF DIXON
>   Is the money still in the car?

EXT. SILVER SEDAN -- THAT MOMENT

The Suspect freezes.

He hadn't noticed. Shit, hadn't even thought about it once he saw his partner's face.

                    THE SUSPECT
                (calling up)
            I'll check.

The chassis creaks and he turns to look back inside the car.

THE SUSPECT'S POV

The duffle bag is a big lump jammed in the corner of the passenger foot well.

                    THE SUSPECT
            It's here!

                    SHERIFF DIXON (O.S.)
                (faint)
            Okay, hook it on, we'll pull it up.

                    THE SUSPECT
            You want me to take this line off? Are you crazy?

                    SHERIFF DIXON (O.S.)
            You're going to have to take it off so we can pull up the car anyway.

                    THE SUSPECT
            Then let's do everything at once!

EXT. RAVINE'S EDGE -- THAT MOMENT

                    SHERIFF DIXON
                (calling down)
            There's a risk of fire in this situation, and I don't know if you're aware of this, Freeman, but currency burns.

                    THE SUSPECT (O.S.)
                (faint)
            I burn, too.

                    SHERIFF DIXON
            That's less of a problem for me.

Off to the side, Deputy Riley smiles at the comment.

                    SHERIFF DIXON
            Listen, we need someone down there to hook the tow line to the car. Like it or not, you're not coming topside until that rustbucket does. So let us get the
                        (MORE)

                    SHERIFF DIXON (CONT'D)
          evidence out nice and careful, the
          evidence that exonerates you, then
          we'll get you and that mess up here.

EXT. SILVER SEDAN -- THAT MOMENT

The Suspect's mind is racing now.

                    THE SUSPECT
               (calling up)
          All right, give me a second. It's kind
          of stuck.

INT. SILVER SEDAN -- MOMENTS LATER

The Suspect crawls past the duffle bag, across to the driver's side.

                    THE SUSPECT
               (low, to himself)
          You can still get out of this.

Crawling over the corpse's back, he works his way over to the two plastic control lever's on the floor by the driver's side door.

One has a gas-tank graphic, the other controls the trunk.

The Suspect twists the trunk lever until it comes off in his hand, leaving just a tiny metal nub.

He crawls back over his partner's body, then stops.

He pulls the keys out of the ignition and pockets them.

EXT. SILVER SEDAN -- MOMENTS LATER

With the duffle bag around one shoulder, the Suspect stands on the door. He takes a deep, calming breath. He's bracing himself for the rush of fear. Below, the ravine disappears into black air.

The Suspect unhooks the winch. He's free. He slips the duffle bag down, wraps the hook around the handles.

                    THE SUSPECT
               (calling up)
          Okay, take it away.

Slowly, the duffle bag rises up, out of his hands. The Suspect keeps his flashlight beam on it.

The Suspect watches it, trying to keep his wits about him.

EXT. RAVINE'S EDGE -- THAT MOMENT

Deputy Riley works the winch controls. The sheriff joins him. They share a look.

FLASH ON --

EXT. BLUE-J MOTEL PARKING LOT -- NIGHT //EARLIER

The sheriff and the deputy talk while the Suspect cools his heels in the back of the Jeep.

> SHERIFF DIXON
> Now you don't have to --

> DEPUTY RILEY
> (interrupting)
> No. I'd want to be a part of that.

> SHERIFF DIXON
> We just have to be aware of the dangers. The risk we're taking on. It's not the kind of risk you agreed to when you took the job.

> DEPUTY RILEY
> Like you said, see where it leads.

> SHERIFF DIXON
> Nothing like this has ever come along in our town. I just need to know where you stand, and know that if things go down suddenly, we're on the same page.

> DEPUTY RILEY
> Definitely.

EXT. RAVINE -- BACK TO SCENE

Dixon gives a cruel smile to his deputy.

> SHERIFF DIXON
> What did I tell you, Edgar?

EXT. SILVER SEDAN -- THAT MOMENT

                    SHERIFF DIXON (O.S.)
              (faint)
          Almighty God made 'em different than
          you and me, and He sure didn't make 'em
          any smarter.

In an instant, the Suspect's vulnerability is thrown into stark relief. He realizes he's built his own trap.

The Suspect doesn't think now, he only acts.

He reaches up to open the rear door, directly above him. It flops open, striking the Suspect hard on the head, but that doesn't slow him down.

He jumps up, getting a grip with both arms.

The hinges creak and groan under his weight. He kicks his legs up, pulling himself to the next level.

The bag keeps moving above him. Out of reach.

The Suspect pulls himself onto the rear windshield, which is nearly as flat a surface as the doors, then jumps again to get to the bumper.

He gets to his feet, balancing on the flat license plate.

On tiptoes, arms outstretched, the duffle bag remains a foot out of reach.

There's only one shot.

The Suspect jumps. His fingers dig into the duffle bag.

His feet leave the rear of the car and then he's in mid-air, getting pulled up. Two feet, three, six...

He holds onto the nylon bag with hands like eagle's talons, but there's no purchase there.

His fingers slip.

The Suspect PLUMMETS almost ten feet, the sedan's rear windshield breaking his fall... and quite possibly his back.

THE SUSPECT'S POV

The duffle bag gets smaller as the winch line is hoisted up. It disappears over the lip of the cliff.

And after a long dark moment, the sheriff's face peers over, looking down at the Suspect like some kind of demon.

> SHERIFF DIXON
> (calling down)
> See... here's the thing, Freeman. No one except Deputy Riley and myself know anything about this recovered money. That puts us in a very interesting position.

TIGHT ON THE SUSPECT

as the ramifications he's facing wash over him.

> THE SUSPECT
> (calling up in a raspy, winded voice)
> Heather knows. She'll dig around, put all this together. She cares and I promise she'll <u>turn</u> on you, I know she will.

TIGHT ON THE SHERIFF

smiling.

> SHERIFF DIXON
> Actually...

FLASH ON --

INT. BLUE-J MOTEL, ROOM 107 -- NIGHT //FLASHBACK//

Sheriff Dixon looks around the empty room. The Motel Receptionist hangs in the doorway.

> SHERIFF DIXON
> Does this phone still work if no one's booked in the room?

> MOTEL RECEPTIONIST
> It's more trouble than it's worth to turn them off.

Dixon picks up the receiver and dials.

> SHERIFF DIXON
> (not really asking)
> Do you suppose I could use it right quick?

The Motel Receptionist shrugs "whatever."

                    OLDER WOMAN (V.O.)
                (through phone)
          Hello?

                    SHERIFF DIXON
                (into phone)
          Heather, please.

                    OLDER WOMAN (V.O.)
          She doesn't want to talk to you.

Thrown, Dixon smiles at the impatient Receptionist.

                    SHERIFF DIXON
          Would you excuse me for a second?
                (after the Receptionist steps
                 outside)
          Sarah, it's Amiel here.

                    OLDER WOMAN (V.O.)
          I know, sheriff.

                    SHERIFF DIXON
          There's some news I thought I should
          share with her. I wouldn't want her
          losing any sleep over the guest we had
          today.

                    OLDER WOMAN (V.O.)
          Mr. Finch.

Dixon is surprised -- annoyed -- that Heather has shared so much information.

                    SHERIFF DIXON
          That's right.

                    OLDER WOMAN (V.O.)
          Heather doesn't want to come to the
          phone.

                    SHERIFF DIXON
          Okay. I respect that. Tell her we heard
          from a towing yard in Cumberland. They
          have a new number since the area code
          change, and Edgar had just been just
          getting a ringing phone all day.

                    OLDER WOMAN (V.O.)
          They towed him all the way to
          Cumberland?

                    SHERIFF DIXON
          Just a mix-up. Please let Heather know
          I checked the car out. His wallet was
          in there. Good ID, real estate flyers,
          the works. Just like he said. I sent
          him on his way back to Chicago with our
          apologies.

                    OLDER WOMAN (V.O.)
          I guess he's not buying that farm.

                    SHERIFF DIXON
          I don't think he'll be buying that one,
          no.

EXT.   RAVINE'S EDGE -- BACK TO SCENE

                    SHERIFF DIXON
               (calling down)
          That's taken care of. Turns out your
          house-hunting story held up. We
          couldn't prove anything, so we let you
          go.
               (laughs at his   accidental
                joke)
          The way you just let go of all that
          money. You almost got back up here. You
          were so close. But see, at the end of
          the day, you can't stick to it. You
          people, there's just no fire in your
          belly.

EXT.   SILVER SEDAN -- THAT MOMENT

                    THE SUSPECT
               (calling up)
          They'll find two bodies.

                    SHERIFF DIXON (O.S.)
               (faint)
          Sure, the guy who pulled the bank job
          had a getaway man. That doesn't mean
          either one was the person in our
          station.
               (beat)
          Don't you know you all look alike?
                    (MORE)

                    SHERIFF DIXON (O.S.) (CONT'D)
            Especially when you're burned beyond
            recognition.

Burned?

Suddenly, Deputy Riley appears at the edge with a red FIVE-GALLON GAS CAN.

                    THE SUSPECT
            No no no.

Riley dumps the fuel -- it falls like rain, splattering all over the sedan's rear end.

                    THE SUSPECT
            You're the police!

                    SHERIFF DIXON
                (calling down)
            Like I told you, Freeman. People can
            surprise you.

FLASH ON --

INT. CELL, MIDLAND TOWNSHIP BUILDING -- DAY //EARLIER//

Dixon sits across from the Suspect.

                    SHERIFF DIXON
            The truth is, there's more going on
            with you than I'll ever know. You're
            smarter than I'm giving you credit for.
            Same goes for me.

EXT.   SILVER SEDAN -- BACK TO SCENE

                    THE SUSPECT
                (shouting up)
            My name's not Freeman.

                    SHERIFF DIXON
                (calling down)
            Now why doesn't that surprise me? Well,
            whoever you are, thanks for the
            retirement present.

The sheriff lets go of his cigar. It tumbles toward the Suspect end-over-end, in slow motion.

There's nothing to do but flinch.

The cigar strikes the license plate and the flames spring to life with a WHOOSH.

The sedan is suddenly lit a hellish orange. The Suspect looks around in some state of amazement. It's come to this.

                THE SUSPECT
        (calling up over the roar of
         the flames)
    Hey Dixon? Dixon? It's been real, man.
    But I just gotta say, you think you're
    on top of this thing? You better hear
    me, 'cause I told you once...

FLASH ON --

INT. CELL, MIDLAND TOWNSHIP BUILDING -- DAY //EARLIER//

Dixon sits across from the Suspect.

                THE SUSPECT
    You have no idea what this
    is about.

EXT.   SILVER SEDAN -- BACK TO SCENE

                THE SUSPECT
        (calling up)
    You have no idea what this
    is about.

The Suspect reaches into his pocket and pulls out the keychain with the sedan's remote control attached.

                THE SUSPECT
    You still don't. Let me show you what
    your big brain did for you.

He thumbs the "TRUNK" button, and the flaming trunk lid flips up, blocking him from the sheriff's view.

In place of looking down at the man he's in the middle of murdering, Sheriff Dixon is now forced to stare at what he's murdering *for*.

A cardboard box filled with money.

Taffy-like strings of burning plastic drip from the lid's tail lights and fall into the trunk.

Dripping into the box.

The money begins to singe. Smoke.

Then BURN.

EXT. RAVINE'S EDGE -- THAT MOMENT

Sheriff Dixon stares down with an expression of utter calm.

                  SHERIFF DIXON
             (to Riley)
        Throw the bag down.

                  DEPUTY RILEY
  What?!

                  SHERIFF DIXON
  You heard me. It's no good.

The deputy looks inside the bag. Wads of cash. Right there.

                  SHERIFF DIXON
        That's nothing but a bag full of
        sorrow. Lord almighty, you think you
        know what you're dealing with...

The sheriff points straight down.

                  SHERIFF DIXON
        You want your share, there it is.

Riley looks over the edge.

RILEY'S POV

The box of money is now ENGULFED IN FLAMES.

The entire situation suddenly locks into focus for Riley.

                  DEPUTY RILEY
        That squirrelly bastard. We're holding
        counterfeit, ain't we?

                  SHERIFF DIXON
        Let it go.

It's unclear whether the sheriff is referring to the money literally, or the entire enraging situation.

Riley interprets it his own way and does as he believes he's been ordered.

He lets the bag go.

FOLLOWING THE FALLING BAG

Tumbling until it hits the --

EXT. SILVER SEDAN -- THAT MOMENT

The duffle bag lands inside the trunk, sending GLOWING EMBERS shooting into the air.

From behind the trunk's lid, the Suspect's dying cackle rings out.

          THE SUSPECT (V.O.)
     And in chess that's what we call a
     stalemate, motherfucker.

EXT. RAVINE'S EDGE -- THAT MOMENT

The sheriff opens up his breast pocket and pulls out the photo he discovered back in the motel room.

It's a school picture of an EIGHT-YEAR-OLD GIRL, a light-skinned African-American.

Gap-toothed, pig-tailed.

He studies it for a beat longer than he needs to, wondering, then flicks it over the edge.

Maybe the flames catch it, maybe the black river does.

                         DISSOLVE TO:

EXT. PORCH, SUBURBAN HOUSE -- MORNING

Shannon signs the Overnight Delivery Man clipboard as he hands her the cardboard envelope.

          OVERNIGHT DELIVERY MAN
     Good morning, ma'am.

The Delivery Man hands her a 9x12 cardboard envelope. She takes it with a smile as thin as the wispy envelope.

              SHANNON
         (considering)
     It is, isn't it...?

INT. FOYER -- THAT MOMENT

Shannon hesitates at the door. Studies the envelope for too long, almost as if she's afraid to learn what's inside.

Then she heads up the stairs.

INT. UPSTAIRS HALLWAY -- MOMENTS LATER

Envelope still in hand, Shannon pauses outside a bedroom door decorated in the cotton-candy pink unicorn and pony world.

She gathers her strength, then enters.

INT. BEDROOM -- THAT MOMENT

Shannon stares down at CALLIE, the girl in the school photo the sheriff found in the motel.

Only now the biracial girl's not smiling. Her face is obscured by a cloudy oxygen mask. She's on major life support, plugged in to archaic tubes and bellows-like ventilating machines.

Yellowed IV bags, monitors something out of the Soviet space program. Weird, desolate home "health" care. End of the line.

On the wall, a DRAWING of a multi-racial family.

                SHANNON
     Honey? Honey?

A momentary hesitation in the wheezing of the machinery. Callie locks eyes with her mother.

                SHANNON
     You remember how I said daddy went for
     help? Remember how I told you he was
     going to go to the ends of the earth to
     find what you need?

                CALLIE
        (muffled, lost)
     Did you hear from daddy?

Tears run down Shannon's cheeks.

Can't speak. She nods. Yes.

INT. MASTER BEDROOM -- MOMENTS LATER

Shannon sits down on her bed, still holding the sealed envelope. Her cheeks streaked with tears, a map of agony.

She goes to open the envelope, but hesitates. Almost as if she's afraid to learn what's inside.

FLASH ON --

INT. GARAGE -- NIGHT //FLASHBACK//

The Suspect and The Bank Robber stare at the slides on the wall: the Bank Robber lost in grief; the Suspect tense, his face a mask of pure determination. But this is a --

NEW ANGLE, REVEALING SHANNON

in the b.g., attentive, but not part of the discussion. Giving her husband room to make his plea.

ANGLE ON THE WALL

revealing the slide images.

-- It's Callie in intensive care --

> THE SUSPECT (O.S.)
> Bottom line, this needs to happen. And if I can't do it, what the fuck's my life worth anyway?

-- It's a shot of the National Organ Donor Registration Waiting List for hearts --

> THE SUSPECT (O.S.)
> Someone on the sixth floor gave me a lead. It's in Argentina.

-- It's the Suspect, leaning against the hospital room door, weeping. CICU Room 613. The <u>sixth floor</u> --

> THE SUSPECT (O.S.)
> Do I really look like the kind of man who's planning on getting himself killed?

INT. MASTER BEDROOM -- BACK TO SCENE

Shannon yanks the pull-tab savagely. The envelope unfolds like a flower.

> THE SUSPECT (V.O.)
> Let's say... whenever you start a new venture, I believe it's wise to make sure you're covered.

A letter from HEARTLAND LIFE INSURANCE CO. slides out, with a CASHIER'S CHECK clipped to it.

Shannon's eyes dance and glisten as she stares at the paper in her hands. The paper that could change her life.

INT. MASTER BEDROOM -- MOMENTS LATER

Shannon sits at the table, holding the phone. The letter sits alone in front of her.

The muted sound the ringing on the other end of the line fills the silent room.

TIGHT SWEEP ON THE LETTER

Depth of field razor-thin, blurring the edges. The check, with <u>a lot of zeros</u>.

> AIRLINE REPRESENTATIVE (V.O.)
> (through phone)
> Heliotrope Airlines Customer Care Relations and Special Services, this is Michele. How may I assist you?

Phrases in cold type:

"HUSBAND..."
   "MISSING, PRESUMED DEAD..."
      "FULL BENEFITS..."
         "DEATH BY MISADVENTURE..."

> SHANNON (V.O.)
> Umm, hi. I'm not sure if you're the right person... I need to arrange international transportation for a... medical patient.

                    AIRLINE REPRESENTATIVE (V.O.)
          Of course, I can help you with that,
          ma'am. Let's start with, what is your
          destination?

MUSIC COMES UP -- Solomon Burke's "None Of Us Are Free" -- as
Shannon struggles to answer the question.

Just a clicking in her dry throat, as if saying it out loud
pulls the trigger on the last bullet of hope left.

                    AIRLINE REPRESENTATIVE (V.O.)
          Ma'am? Your destination?

But finally:

                    SHANNON (V.O.)
          Argentina.

                                                CUT TO BLACK.

                          THE END

CAST AND CREW CREDITS

MODOC SPRING presents
a STUART CONNELLY picture

THE SUSPECT

MEKHI PHIFER   WILLIAM SADLER

STERLING K. BROWN   JAMES McCAFFREY   REBECCA CRESKOFF

Written and Directed by
STUART CONNELLY

Produced by

ROBYN K. BENNETT   MARY JO BARTHMAIER   STUART CONNELLY   SCOTT C. ARONSON

Executive Producers

MEKHI PHIFER   THOMAS & ANNA MARIE CANNIERE   PAUL & KATHLEEN BARTHMAIER   MICHAEL & TRACY BOLLAG

JEFFREY R. BOYLE   BRENT BUCK & KATIE BARTHMAIER   JOE & JENNIFER GALEA   W. ROBERT & PAMELA J. LANDIS

DINA ENGEL & SHERRY McCRACKEN   RAPHAEL CHE

Co-Producer	Associate Producer	Co-Producer
PAUL BARTHMAIER	MAUREEN KELLEY McKENNA	CHAD SCHEIFELE

Casting by	Costume Designer	Production Designer	VFX Supervisor
CAROLINE SINCLAIR	SOFIA MESICEK	EILEEN DENNEHY	MO FORKER

Director of Photography	Editor	Composer	Music by
ERIC GIOVON	RAY CHUNG	STEPHEN COATES	THE REAL TUESDAY WELD

A MODOC SPRING / BURIED LEDE PRODUCTION

CAST

Express Delivery Man .... Anthony Panichelli	Polaski Patrol Car Driver .... David J. Bonner
Shannon .... Rebecca Creskoff	Polaski Patrol Car Partner .... Brian Gligor
Sheriff Dixon .... William Sadler	Bank Manager .... Randy Miller
Heather .... Lizzy DeClement	Truck Driver .... Denny Bess
Deputy Riley .... Derek Roché	Truck Driver's Girlfriend .... Carla Corvo
The Suspect .... Mekhi Phifer	Cashier .... Mark Barthmaier
The Other Suspect .... Sterling K. Brown	Motel Receptionist .... Marisa Brown
Meredith .... Bernadette Quigley	Lab Volunteer .... Megan Corry
Maid .... Louise Devery	Lab Proctor .... Jennie Eisenhower
Polaski Sheriff .... James McCaffrey	Psychology Test Subject .... Mike Mergo
First Polaski Cop .... James Bagnell	Printer .... Luke Robertson
Second Polaski Cop .... Michael Fallon	Callie .... Madison Zamor

VOICEOVER TALENT

Radio Anchor .... Stuart Connelly
Motel Operator .... Maureen Kelley McKenna
Mrs. Noble .... Mary Jo Barthmaier
Airline Representative .... Nicole Agostino

CREW

Coordinating Producers .... Renee Panichelli
                                          Lamese Williams
Unit Production Manager .... Aliki Paraschis
First Assistant Director .... Maureen Kelley McKenna
Second Assistant Director .... Nicole Agostino
Script Supervisor .... Charles S. Rowe
Accountant .... Lorraine Hawk
Accounting Clerk .... Cassandra Bressler
Production Coordinator .... Samantha Hatfield
Assistant Production Office Coordinator .... Alex Levin
Office PA .... Kelly Beiler
Second Second Assistant Director .... Tim Bradley
Key Set PA .... Chris Wright Jr.
First Team PA .... Leah Spicer
Walkie PA .... Keith Eyrich
Production Assistants .... Stephen Litten
            David L. Powell III, Jo Anna Van Thuyne
            Luke Marron, Courtney Fusselman
First Assistant Camera .... Rebecca Rajadnya
Second Assistant Camera / DIT .... Jeff Clanet
Still Photographer .... Sherry McCracken
Jib Operator .... Abad Rosa
Sound Mixer .... Matt Martin
Boom Operator .... Paul Padilla
Gaffer .... Jon Carr
Best Boy Electric .... Joe Del Balzo, Brandon Roberts
Electric .... Kyle Rebar
Key Grip .... John F. Draus
Best Boy Grip .... Andrew Joffe
Grips .... Steve Cameron, Dave Ruth, Greg Roth, Jim Tripp
Property Master .... Mark Barthmaier
Art Director .... Danielle Payne
Set Dresser .... Kathryn Burkholder
Set Decorator .... Jon Giancola
Construction Coordinator .... Karl Snyder
Art PA .... Mike Kerbaugh
Scenic .... Katie Schwartz
Graphic Designer .... Brent Buck
Original Artwork provided by .... Madeline Kelly,
            Wesley Connelly, Callie Connelly
Storyboard Artist .... Chad Scheifele
Wardrobe Supervisor .... Amber Givens
Key Hair and Make Up .... Claudia Seyler
Assistant Hair and Make Up .... Paula Graffunder
Location Managers .... Paul T. Barthmaier, Katrina Weidman
Stunt Consultant .... Tim Gallin
Stunt Performer .... Maurice "Reese" Davis
Add'l Stunt Drivers .... Robyn K. Bennett, David L. Powell III
Harley Wrangler .... Edgar Schlimmie
Police Vehicle Wrangler .... Randy Miller
Process Trailer .... Neal Weaver

Eileen Martin .... Craft Services
Assistant Editor .... Dean McKenna

SECOND UNIT

Director of Photography .... David Kruta
First Assistant Camera .... Ian Mosley-Duffy
Second Assistant Camera / DIT .... Max Tubman, Spencer Zabiela
Still Photographer .... Anthony Fabrikant
Sound Mixer .... Johnpaul Golaski
Boom Operator .... Maxwell Cooke
Gaffer .... Dominic Sivilli
Grip .... Gabriel Harris
Property Assistant .... Seymour Levin
Scenic .... Robin Pinch
Graphic Designer .... Lisa Basil
Wardrobe Supervisor .... Lauren Rothery
Set Costumer .... Rita Squitiere
Assistant Hair and Make Up .... Theresa Nyugen
Assistant Make Up .... Nora Fitzgerald
Script Supervisor .... Roy Koriakin
Second Assistant Director .... Blair Howley
Second Second Assistant Director .... Quinn Doherty
Key Set PA .... Mike Bush
Production Coordinator .... Kate Diesinger
Production Assistants .... Deborah Kofsky, Brendan Zoltowski,
            Kyle Hamilton
Visual Effects and Intermediate by DIVE
2D Supervisor .... Rueben Rodas
Compositors .... Matthew "Boston" Robertson,
            Anton Moss, Joe DiValerio
Matte Painter .... Shannan Burkley
Paint Artists .... Matthew Burres, Mark Longchamps
Matchmover .... Drew Beekler
Visual Effects Editor .... Ben Updegrove
Visual Effects Executive Producer .... Bob Lowery
Visual Effects/DI Producer .... Andy Williams
Visual Effects Coordinator .... Jennifer Wessner
DI Colorist .... Alex Bickel
DI Color Consultant .... MO Forker
DI Conforming Editor .... Bryan Baker
Main Titles .... Matthew Burres
End Titles .... Kevin Fanning
Additional Visual Effects Artist .... Grover L. Richardson III
Visual Effects Pyrotechnician .... Jeffrey Cox
Pyrotechnics Assistants .... John Spatrino, Joe Fuglio
Visual Effects Camera Operator .... Kevin Hackenberg
Visual Effects Camera Assistant .... Adam Bogus
Additional Visual Effects Camera Assistants .... Eric Cicale,
            Paul Dampier, Mitch McClure
Visual Effects Storyboard Artist .... Malcolm McNeill
Dialogue Editor .... Dan Korintus
Sound Effects Editor .... Scott Waz, CAS
Foley Artists .... Sandra Fox, Goro Koyama
Foley Recording Mixer .... Jack Heeren
Foley Recordist .... Stephen Muir
Sound Supervisor .... Scott Waz, CAS
Re-Recording Mixer .... John Baker

Foley recorded at Footsteps Post-Production Sound Inc.
Mixed at Philadelphia Post a Dream Out Loud company, Inc.
Insurance Services provided by Film Emporium
Legal Services provided by Law Office of Scott C. Aronson

ATHESIST TOWN
Written by Stephen Coates and Joe Coles
Performed by The Real Tuesday Weld
Produced by The Clerkenwell Kid

HAPPY ENDINGS
Written by Stephen Coates
Performed by The Real Tuesday Weld
Produced by The Clerkenwell Kid

BLACKBIRD DAY
Written by Stephen Coates and Joe Coles
Performed by The Real Tuesday Weld
Produced by The Clerkenwell Kid

This project was made possible with the support of the Commonwealth of Pennsylvania and the Pennsylvania Film Office
Assistance was provided by the Greater Philadelphia Film Office
Invaluable guidance and support provided by Sharon Pinkenson, Executive Director Greater Philadelphia Film Office

The Suspect was filmed entirely on location in Pennsylvania

The Producers wish to thank the following for their generous support and assistance:
  Asher's Chocolate
  Brookville Glove Mfg.
  Kobold Watch Co.
  Twin Valley Coffee Co.
  Yuengling Beer
  Zippo Lighters
  Pennsylvania Pure Distilleries,
    makers of Boyd and Blair® Potato Vodka
  The people of Elverson Borough, West Nantmeal
    and Caernarvon Townships
  Chief Paul Stoltz and the Caernarvon Police Department
  Twin Valley Fire Department, Station 69
  Berks Homes, The Springfield Village in Elverson
  The rangers of French Creek State Park
  Mary K. Dougherty, Mary K. Dougherty and Associates
  Mia Colona, Nicole Miller Philadelphia
  Brian Barthmaier and his friends at Centurion Motor Cars
  Gary Elston, The Petsmith Company
  Ludwig's Grille & Oyster Bar
  Firecreek Restaurant & Bar
  Marilyn & Nelson Beam
  West Nantmeal Township Board of Supervisors
  East Nantmeal Board of Supervisors
  Gawthrop Greenwood, PC
  Morgantown Reuzit Shoppe
  Hallman's General Store, Chester Springs
  Quality Inn, Pottstown
  Journal Register Offset, Exton

St. Mary of Providence Center, Elverson
Elverson Borough Council
Boy Scout Troop 37, Elverson
The Red Carpet Inn, Morgantown
Joanna's General Store, Morgantown
Rich Orlow, Piazza Management
Randy DiLibero, Ramjin Holdings
Susquehanna Bank, Morgantown Branch
Holiday Inn, Morgantown
Yorgey's National Uniform Rental
SOS Copiers
Lost Soul Picture Cars
Karen Speicher
Sarah Copp
Russell Miller
Kathleen Nelson
Mike Royce

And special thanks to Sharon Pinkenson for her love of film, filmmakers and Philadelphia

© 2013 THE SUSPECT LLC

The story, all names, characters and incidents portrayed in this production are fictitious. No identification with actual persons, places, buildings or products is intended or should be inferred.

All material is protected by Copyright Laws of the United States and all countries throughout the world. All rights reserved.

Any unauthorized exhibition, distribution or copying of this film or any part thereof (including the soundtrack) is an infringement of the relevant copyright and will subject the infringer to severe civil and criminal penalties.

RELEASED BY IMAGE ENTERTAINMENT

Licensed internationally through ITN DISTRIBUTION
Contact: meetings@itndistribution.com

www.thesuspectmovie.com

www.ingramcontent.com/pod-product-compliance
Lightning Source LLC
Chambersburg PA
CBHW081506040426
42446CB00017B/3419